Dyslexia Tools Workbook for Teens

Dyslexia Tools

Workbook for Teens

120 Exercises to Improve Reading Skills

Dr. Gavin Reid and Jenn Clark

ROCKRIDGE PRESS

We wish to acknowledge, first and foremost, all young people with dyslexia for their determination and strengths. Also, their teachers and parents, who tirelessly seek best practices to help young people with dyslexia. Additionally, we wish to acknowledge our colleagues for their insights and support.

Interior and Cover Designer: John Clifford
Art Producer: Sue Bischofberger
Editor: Andrea Leptinsky
Production Editor: Matt Burnett
Production Manager: Riley Hoffman

Images used under license from Shutterstock.com

ISBN: Print 978-1-64876-921-4 | eBook 978-1-64876-264-2
R0

Contents

For Parents and Teachers

Welcome to the *Dyslexia Tools Workbook for Teens*! This book contains a range of activities to help teens with dyslexia develop and consolidate their reading and learning skills. It is not a book for very young children, nor for beginning readers, but rather for teens who are already reading at a basic level but still below their grade level. We can relate to this and to the frustrations of experiencing reading challenges with dyslexia. Young people eagerly converse about what is currently trending in their teenage orbit, and usually there are some books involved. Most trends—whether in sports, music, or fashion—often involve access to print, causing the student with dyslexia to feel left out. During this time, they can become quite adept at pretending, specifically pretending to read. Politely, this may be referred to as a compensatory strategy, one that they may utilize for many years.

The trends when we were teens are different from the ones today, but knowledge of trends represents access to popularity and inclusion. Today, trends can include accessing sophisticated technology, contributing on social media, or participating in fantasy football leagues. One might wonder, then, where reading fits into all this. Reading is the gateway, and it represents the path that can take young people where they want to go.

Dyslexia Tools Workbook for Teens aims to equip teenagers ages 12 to 16 with the tools of reading, the skills of problem solving, and the resilience to survive as they go through middle and high school.

This book consists of activities that will help students move from a basic level of reading to a higher level by acquiring reading fluency and a higher level of comprehension. The activities are developed to promote independent working, but there are suggestions for ways parents and teachers can support a young person using this book. The workbook should be seen as an accompanying resource to a reading program. The activities will be broadly based on the Orton-Gillingham approach in that the book contains activities that are explicit, sequential, and systematic in breaking reading and writing into smaller skills involving letters and sounds. There is clear evidence-based research indicating that the Orton-Gillingham approach, used widely in schools in the United States and Canada, can represent the gold standard in teaching reading.

We hope you find this a useful tool to help you and your child or student develop key skills toward reading mastery.

For Teens

We are delighted you have decided to use this workbook! This decision is a really positive step, and we know it isn't easy to try to deal with challenges. We hope this book will be fun and enjoyable and help you along the road to success. Taking responsibility for your own learning will also help you develop your own learning strategies. Remember, what works for someone else might not work for you. We are all different!

One purpose of this book is to give you independence in developing reading and learning skills so you can succeed in middle or high school, the next stages in your education, and eventually, your career. You are laying the foundations for these next stages now, and this book will help you do so in a positive and fun way.

Yes, dyslexia can be challenging, but we believe it is a challenge that you will be able to deal with and eventually overcome. However, to get there, you need to develop skills in reading fluently and strategies to help with memorizing, learning, and studying. There are 120 fun activities in this book, as well as sections with tips and tools for managing your dyslexia in every subject and in your personal life.

You don't need to complete the activities in order, but they are in a sequence. They start with some review activities from earlier learning and move on to activities that are more challenging. You can note your own progress as the answers are at the back of the book. Finding out where and how you made a mistake is very important. Don't be discouraged if you don't get all the answers correct! This book is a learning tool. We don't expect you will get everything correct. We want you to learn from these activities so that you can use this knowledge when you are learning new material, reviewing for tests and exams, and reading for pleasure.

We are excited to share this book, and we want to share that excitement with you! We've tried to make the activities relate to what you and your friends might enjoy. The exercises are designed with fun and, at times, humor in mind. We really hope you enjoy this activity book and can use it to enrich your school experience and make the most of your skills and abilities. We have worked in the area of dyslexia for many years and have seen teens like yourself flourish, develop amazing creative talents, and become very successful. This brings us great joy, and we hope this book helps you in the same way. Dyslexia is not a barrier to success!

Phonics and Phonemic Awareness

1. Vowels vs. Consonants

This activity helps you practice spotting vowels (A, E, I, O, U) and consonants.

For the following list of famous people, write all the vowels in each name in one column, and all the consonants in the other column. The first one is done for you as an example.

Famous Person	Vowels in Their Name (A, E, I, O, U)	Consonants in Their Name
Will Smith	ii	wll smth
Tom Hanks		
Morgan Freeman		
Miley Cyrus		
Lady Gaga		
Justin Bieber		
Mariah Carey		
Justin Timberlake		
Leonardo DiCaprio		
Michael Jordan		
Missy Elliott		
Dwayne Johnson		
Sandra Bullock		
Kanye West		
Eddie Murphy		
Adam Sandler		
Samuel L. Jackson		
Jennifer Aniston		

2. Make the Syllable

It is important to be able to hear the syllables (sometimes called "parts" or "beats") in a word. This helps you break apart longer words while reading. You might need to say the word out loud if you don't hear the parts or beats in your head. For this activity, you'll be focusing on the syllables you hear. Remember, this is about hearing the parts or beats, not the letters!

For example, the first image is of headphones. When you say it out loud, you hear "head/phones" (two syllables), so you would draw two dots.

3. Take a Break

Looking at the positions involved in defense in football, break each name down into syllables using a forward slash—for example, de/fense. Then, write each word on its appropriate line beneath the chart.

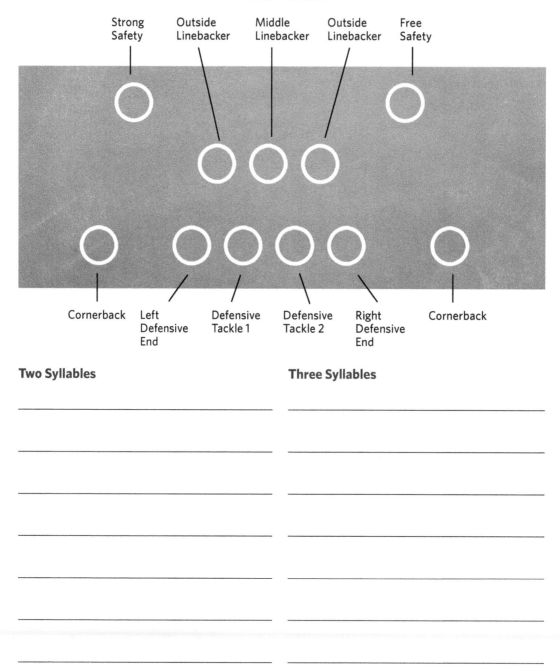

Football Defense

Strong Safety Outside Linebacker Middle Linebacker Outside Linebacker Free Safety

Cornerback Left Defensive End Defensive Tackle 1 Defensive Tackle 2 Right Defensive End Cornerback

Two Syllables

_____

_____

_____

_____

_____

Three Syllables

_____

_____

_____

_____

_____

4. Blend the Positions

In the table below, the positions from the football offense diagram have been broken into syllables. Blend the syllables together to make the word. The first two are done for you. Please note that some of the words only have two syllables.

1st Syllable	2nd Syllable	3rd Syllable	*Whole Word*
back	field		*backfield*
tack	le		*tackle*
cen	ter		
quar	ter	back	
foot	ball		
re	ceiv	er	
scrim	mage		
run	ning		
of	fen	sive	

Football Offense

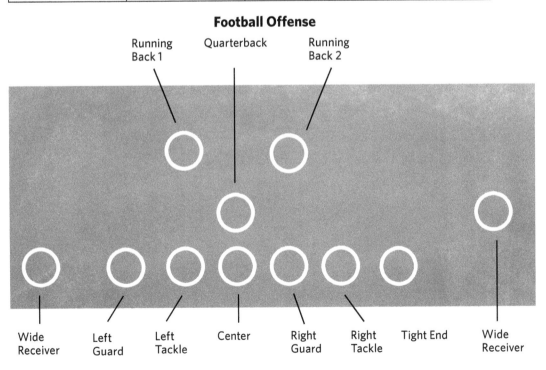

Running Back 1   Quarterback   Running Back 2

Wide Receiver   Left Guard   Left Tackle   Center   Right Guard   Right Tackle   Tight End   Wide Receiver

5. Rhyme Production

Complete the four rhymes below. Use whatever words you want here!

- Joe sat on the bank of the stream on a log;

  - he was sure the small green blob below was a _____.

- The firefighter picked up the hose;

  - quickly the water jetted over his face and _____.

- The smoothie Dana ordered was terribly late,

  - and she was really upset that she had to _____.

- The football coach said as a player, Larry was a dream.

  - So, he thought, why was I not chosen for the _____?

6. Match the Rhymes

Draw lines to match the words with their rhyming partners.

Neat	Shark
Bark	Sick
Crumpet	Pair
Chick	Quick
Care	Apple
Grapple	Trumpet
Flick	Meet
Rug	Cookie
Looter	Bangle
Boot	Suit
Crew	Computer
Took	Mug
Bun	Score
Angle	Fun
Goal	Soul
Rookie	Look
More	Brew

7. Songs and Rhymes

Rhyming can occur in different types of texts like poems and songs. You can hear rhymes by listening for the same or similar sounds at the end of a word. It's fun to notice rhymes in songs! Spot the rhyming words in this traditional folk song "Danny Boy," written by Frederic Weatherly. Take a look at the first four lines:

>**Oh, Danny Boy, the pipes, the pipes are <u>calling</u>**
>**From glen to glen, and down the mountain <u>side</u>.**
>**The summer's gone, and all the roses <u>falling</u>.**
>**It's you, it's you must go, and I must <u>abide</u>.**

In these lines, the words "calling" and "falling" rhyme, and "side" and "abide" rhyme. Notice that these paired words sound the same at the end of the words.

Look up the lyrics online and mark all the rhyming words or phrases. Then, choose your own favorite song and do the same with the lyrics.

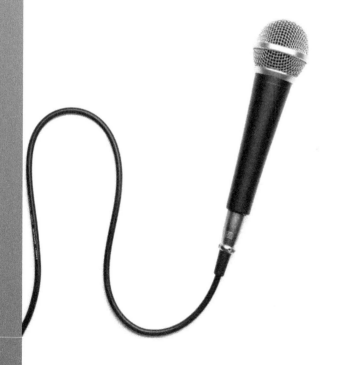

8. Draw the Rhyme

Rhyming words have the same sound at the end, like "hair" and "chair."

Now, write a rhyming word that matches the target word. Then, draw an emoji of the word.

Target Word	Rhyming Word	Emoji
hair	*bear*	
red		
goal		
boat		
train		

9. Common Vowel Patterns

Vowel combinations have two vowels together that form the sound of the first letter. For example, AI in "pain" sounds like the letter A, and EA in "beat" sounds like the letter E. Use the clues to help you write the other words.

Vowel Pattern	Clue	Word
AY	Have a good one!	
AY	The month before June	
EA	A treat is to _____	
AI	It falls from the sky	
EE	Arranging to see friends	
OA	Body wash	soap
OA	A sailor sails in a _____	

10. Vowel Patterns

Short vowels are vowel sounds in which the letters A, E, I, O, and U make a short sound—for example, /a/ in "sat," /e/ in "pet," /i/ in "sit," /o/ in "lot," and /u/ in "bus."

Long vowels say their own letter names. Long vowel sounds are formed by putting two vowels together or by using a vowel-consonant E pattern.

Below is a list of words with short vowels. Make them into long vowels either by replacing a vowel, adding an extra vowel in the middle (ran → rain), or by adding a silent E at the end of a word (tap → tape). Make sure that they are real words by writing a sentence or phrase using the word with a long vowel sound. Here are some of the more common vowel combinations you can use: AI, AY, EE, EA, OA, OW, IGH.

Short Vowel	Long Vowel	Sentence or Phrase Using the Long Vowel Word
bat		
sad		
twin		
bit		
cub		

11. Short Vowels

Try turning these long vowels into short ones.

Long Vowel	Short Vowel	Sentence That Has the Short Vowel
tube		
cane		
main		
plane		
dime		

12. **Short and Long U**

The vowel U can be tricky! In the chart below, turn the short U into a long U by adding a silent E to the end of the word.

Short U	Long U
dud	
mut	
cut	
us	
tub	

Now do the opposite by removing the silent E.

Long I	Short I
pipe	
kite	
bite	
stripe	
mite	

13. Beat the Clock

This activity will help you practice your long and short vowels. This will be important for spelling activities later in the book.

Circle the long vowel words and put a square around the short vowel words. See how many you can circle or square in 120 seconds (two minutes). Remember, a long vowel sounds like its letter name!

clock	cuff	ant	shrug	vet	zoo	lean	us
pup	muck	weak	score	home	duck	gut	stump
truck	fume	him	wimp	pug	sum	plus	suit
Pete	cup	lead	vote	pen	June	zen	muck
cub	deal	sell	blast	bean	game	duck	track
peek	shrub	wet	main	luck	hut	feel	beg
tell	jean	hem	lose	hum	den	pun	yet
glue	open	fruit	gum	goal	shrimp	Jen	yes
jug	mute	nut	seal	fuss	lump	coal	rut

14. Blend It Up

A consonant blend is when two or more consonants are blended together but each sound can be heard in the blend. For example, if you see SN together in a word, the /s/ is blended with the /n/. You can hear the sound for each letter, but the sounds are blended together. Blends can occur at the beginning or end of a word. In this activity, try to create as many real consonant blends as you can think of. Be careful! Make sure you are blending consonants that produce a real sound. The first two are done as an example.

Single Consonant	Single Consonant	Single Consonant	Blends (Make As Many As You Can)	Word Using This Blend
S	T	R	ST, STR, TR	stop, strip, trip
C	L	R	CL, CR	clap, crust
F	T	R		
B	L	R		
T	R	S		
F	L	R		
G	L	R		
T	R	S		
S	P	T		
S	M	P		
R	P	F		

15. Track the Blend

Make your own words from these 20 beginning consonant blends. It's a race!

START >	BL	SM	CR	PL	ST
					SC
	TR	SP	BR	GL	FR
	FL				
	CL	PR	TW	SW	SN
					GR
			FINISH	PR	DR

16. **Consonant Digraphs**

Consonant digraphs are created by combining two consonants to make a new sound.
For example, the letters SH together make the one sound /sh/.

Some common consonant digraphs are SH, CH, CK, and WH.

Fish: SH is a consonant digraph

Bench: CH is a consonant digraph

When: WH is a consonant digraph

Truck: CK is a consonant digraph

Look at the following pictures and write down the digraph that corresponds with each one.
The first two have been done for you.

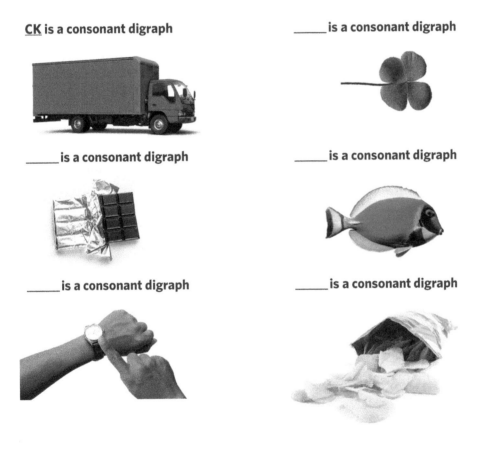

CK is a consonant digraph

_____ **is a consonant digraph**

_____ **is a consonant digraph**

_____ **is a consonant digraph**

_____ **is a consonant digraph**

_____ **is a consonant digraph**

17. Blends vs. Digraphs

Although consonant blends and digraphs are both made of consonants, they are different. A consonant blend is when two or more consonants are blended together but each sound may be heard in the blend. For example, in the word "scrap," the first three consonants, SCR, are a consonant blend because the individual sounds /s/, /c/, and /r/can be heard. Blends can be found at the beginning or end of a word.

Consonant digraphs are created by combining two or more consonants, but the letter combination makes only one sound. For example, in the word "shape," the first two consonants, SH, only make the one sound /sh/. Like blends, consonant digraphs can be found either at the beginning or the end of a word.

In this activity, you will make up two different teams, Consonant Digraph Team and Consonant Blend Team. Use the **last name** of each player to sort them into the team that matches the consonant pattern in their name.

Your Choice of Players:

Simpson Flash	**Sean Meesh**
Sean Seesh	**Ivan Drodge**
Phillip Sketch	**Tim Dereck**
Stone Drummond	**Will Smith**
Brian Blast	**Chad Whendle**
Holms Frond	**Paul Vestrand**

Consonant Digraph Team	Consonant Blend Team
Meesh	Drummond

18. **Sound Deletion**

Sound deletion is figuring out how a word would sound if a part of the word, like a sound or syllable, was deleted. For example, with the word "airplane," take away the first syllable ("air"), and the syllable remains "plane."

For this exercise, write the word under the picture. Then, remove the first syllable and write what is left.

Whole Word	Second Syllable or Sound
airplane	plane
_____	_____
_____	_____
_____	_____

19. Final Sound Detection

In this activity, listen for the final sound in each word. Say the name of the item in the picture and write only the final sound. For example, say the word "coffee." The final sound is a long E, so write "/e/" in the second column. For the last two rows, pick your own words.

20. Take the Pop Quiz!

Congratulations on finishing the activities in this section. Now it's time to see what you learned. Read the following questions and pick the best answer.

1. What is a consonant?

   a. a letter in the alphabet

   b. something you find in alphabet soup

   c. a letter in the alphabet that is not A, E, I, O, or U

2. A consonant digraph is _____.

   a. two letters that make two sounds

   b. two letters that make one sound

   c. a picture of a letter

3. Words that rhyme have _____.

   a. different sounds at the end

   b. the same spelling

   c. the same sound at the end of the word

4. An E at the end of the word usually makes the middle vowel say _____.

   a. its short name

   b. nothing

   c. its long name or its letter name

5. A consonant blend is _____.

   a. when a combination of consonants are blended together but the sounds of each letter can be heard

   b. tons of consonants

   c. two or three letters that make one sound

➡

6. Which letter combination is a blend?

    a. III

    b. SH

    c. SPL

7. Which vowels can say a long E sound?

    a. EA, EE

    b. AI, AY

    c. OI, OW

8. Words that rhyme have the same spelling at the end of the word.

    a. true

    b. false

9. How many syllables are in the word "window"?

    a. 3

    b. 5

    c. 2

10. SH is a consonant digraph.

    a. true

    b. false

Syllables and Multiple-Syllable Words

21. Count the Syllables

It's important to recognize the difference between sounds and syllables. A sound can be referred to as a phoneme, which is quite different from a syllable. A sound (phoneme) is the smallest unit in speech. For example, the word "bat" has three sounds (phonemes): /b/, /a/, and /t/. A syllable is a cluster of sounds, and it must have at least one vowel. For example, the word "bat" has a vowel and is only one syllable.

For this activity, count the syllables and divide the word into syllable parts. This might be a review, but it will help develop what is called automaticity, which means being able to do something automatically. At first, you might need to think about it, but as you practice, you will be able to do it automatically and more quickly.

For each picture, count the number of syllables, then write the word showing the different syllables. For example, for a picture of a watermelon, you would write **4: wa/ter/mel/on**.

Picture	Number of Syllables	Syllable Parts

22. **Silly Syllables**

Being able to identify syllables is important for accurate reading and for reading fluency. Fluent reading helps with reading comprehension. For this activity, count the syllables and divide the word into syllable parts. The words are nonsense words, which makes it more difficult, but the same rules apply as with real words.

Show the parts of each word with a forward slash mark (/). The first one is done as an example. Hint: Each syllable has one vowel sound.

Word	Number of Syllables	Syllable Parts
estaboric	4	es/ta/bor/ic
yogonda		
barrasa		
wundolul		
farinic		
sotepic		
toreptic		
pranafam		
jogilic		
anermas		
trepal		
sastac		
lulocal		
preham		

23. The Six Types of Syllables

There are not just one, or two types of syllables—but six! Let's take a look.

1. **Closed Syllables:** This is when the vowel is followed by one or more consonants. The vowel is short. For example, "but" is a closed syllable because the T follows the U.

2. **Open Syllables:** An open syllable has a single vowel that is at the end of the word or syllable. The vowel is long. For example, the word "me" is an open syllable because there is one vowel and no consonant to close in the vowel.

3. **Consonant + LE Syllables:** These are found only at the end of words, like "table" and "puzzle." If a consonant + LE syllable is combined with an open syllable, there is no double consonant in the word. For example, in the word "table," the first syllable (ta/ble) is open, so the next consonant in the word is not doubled.

4. **Vowel/Consonant/E Syllables:** Magic E is another name for this syllable type. When there is a silent E at the end of a word, the middle vowel is long. One example is the word "time." The vowel in the middle is long, and the E at the end is not pronounced.

5. **R-Controlled Syllables:** When a vowel is followed by an R, it colors or changes the sound the vowel makes. For example, in the word "tar," the AR sounds like the letter R. This can apply to any vowel that is controlled by an R, such as the OR in "doctor" or the AR in "car."

6. **Vowel Team Syllables:** This is when two vowels together make one vowel sound, such as EE in "beep," EA in "bean," or AI in "rain."

In the chart below, write three examples of each vowel type.

Syllable Type	Example 1	Example 2	Example 3
Closed Syllables			
Open Syllables			
Consonant + LE Syllables			
Vowel/Consonant/E Syllables			
R-Controlled Syllables			
Vowel Team Syllables			

24. Closed Syllables

A closed syllable is when the vowel is short and closed off at the end by one or more consonants. When the vowel is closed in by a consonant, it can say its short vowel name. For example, in the word "bet," the T closes in the E, so it is a short vowel.

In the chart, circle the vowels in the word, then decide if the word is closed or not closed and put a check mark in the appropriate column.

Word	Yes: Closed Syllable	No: Not a Closed Syllable
blast	✔	
hi		
snap		
me		
met		
truck		
she		
flat		
it		
he		
shrimp		

25. **Spot the Open Syllable**

An open syllable is a single vowel that says its long name at the end of a word or a syllable. For example, the word "me" is an open syllable. The vowel is at the end of the word, so there is not a consonant to close the syllable. In a multisyllabic word like "spider" (spi/der), the I is long because no consonants close in the vowel at the end of the first syllable.

Understanding the difference between closed and open syllables will help you read unknown words and decide how to pronounce the vowel sound. In this activity, you need to spot the open syllables. Circle only the open syllable words.

music	sped	she	blend
decide	depend	shrimp	begin
nest	glad	silo	best
be	drifting	invest	me
dust	I	draft	include
delay	maze	open	help
rust	halo	jump	tiger

26. Consonant + LE Syllable

Many common words have a consonant + LE combination. (Tip: Consonant + LE is always its own syllable, so you always make a syllable break before it.)

Steps for Identifying Consonant + LE

Read the following steps and see how they work with the word "bangle."

1. Find the vowels. b<u>a</u>ngl<u>e</u> (A and E)

2. Is there an E at the end of the word? b<u>a</u>ngl<u>e</u> (yes)

3. Check to see there is LE at the end. bang<u>le</u> (yes)

4. If LE is at the end, then split the word before the consonant. ban/gle

5. Read the syllables. The first syllable ends with a consonant, so it is a short vowel sound.

6. The second syllable says the /gl/ sound, and the E is silent.

An example of an open syllable + consonant + LE would be "ta/ble." There is no consonant closing the vowel, so it is a long vowel A.

Below, make a list of six words with a consonant + LE at the end. Then, divide the words into syllables (such as han/dle). In the third column, write whether the first vowel is long or short.

Words	Syllables	Long/Short First Vowel

27. The Magic E Syllable

You will find many words with the Magic E. It is called Magic E because the E is silent. When this happens, the vowel that comes before it makes the sound of its letter name, or the long vowel sound. The following examples have short vowel sounds. If an E is added to the end, the vowel becomes long and sounds like the name of the letter.

- cub + E = cube
- tub + E = tube
- pan + E = pane
- rob + E = robe

For this exercise, imagine all the items you and your friend, Jane, might see when you go out for a fun day. Don't forget, the items must have a Magic (silent) E.

You leave the house and go to the bakery. Then you go to the deli to get a smoothie. You meet your friend, Jane, and you both go to the game at your school. Your team wins. Then, you meet your older brother, and he drives you both home.

Word	Where Did You See It?	Sentence or Phrase

28. R-Controlled Syllables

An R-controlled syllable is when the R controls the vowel sound. It is sometimes called the Bossy R, because the R tells the vowel what sound to make. In many short words with one vowel in the middle, the vowel has a short vowel sound—for example, "cat" and "fat." If you replace the last letter of each of these words with the letter R, the sound of the vowel changes. For example, "cat" becomes "car," and "fat" becomes "far."

Examples of words with R-controlled vowels are shown below. Think of more words to complete the table.

AR	ER	IR	OR	UR
hard	over	skirt	storm	purple
far	better	flirt	more	curl

29. Vowel Team Syllables

A vowel team syllable has two vowels next to each other that, together, make one sound. "M<u>ou</u>th," "r<u>ai</u>n," and "b<u>oa</u>t," for example, all contain vowel teams. The two different kinds of vowel teams are vowel digraphs and diphthongs (sliding sounds). Examples of vowel digraphs are the vowel teams AI, AY, EE, EY, OA, and OE. These vowel team digraphs make one sound, usually the long vowel sound of the first letter in the vowel team. Diphthongs are a type of vowel digraph, but the vowel sound within a diphthong glides. This means that it starts off as one vowel sound and glides into a different vowel sound. For example, when you say the word "cow," the vowel starts off as /ow/ but ends with more of a /w/ sound. Diphthongs also make one sound, but it is a new sound.

For this activity, make up your own ridiculous ranch. Draw what it would look like in the open space below. List all the items/animals you might see on a ranch that have vowel teams in their names. For example, in the word "cow," the vowel team is OW. In the word "mouse," the vowel team is OU. They both say /ow/ but are spelled differently.

30. Syllable Division: Where to Divide Words

Syllable division may seem challenging at first, but once you are able to master it, reading and spelling will become easier. Being able to divide words into syllables can help you read longer words more easily and speed up your reading. Syllable division can also help you spell words, because if you can break the word into smaller units, you can sound it out. This is really helpful for longer (multisyllabic) words.

There are five types of syllable division. (Note: In this list, "V" stands for vowel, and "C" stands for consonant.)

1. Rab/bit

This is a **VC/CV** word.

2. Po/ny

This is a **V/CV** word. (Remember, Y is a vowel when it comes at the end of a word.)

3. Rob/in

This is a **VC/V** word.

4. Mon/ster

This is a **VC/CCV** word. Note that for this type, a consonant can shift to become a **VCC/CV** word (like pump/kin). This depends on where the blend, or consonant digraph, is.

5. Li/on

This is a **CV/VC** word.

Practice with the five types of syllable division using the following table. Divide each word into syllables, then write which of the five types it relates to. The first one is completed for you.

Word	Division	Syllable Type
metal	met/al	robin
hotel		
dentist		
poet		
complex		
contest		

31. **Five Types of Syllable Division: Rabbit**

"Rabbit" is a VC/CV word. Follow these steps to divide this word type.

- Look at the word "rabbit." Under the word, mark the letters as vowels (V) or consonants (C). Start at the first vowel.

RABBIT

_____

- Keep marking until you meet another vowel, then stop. Only mark vowel to vowel.

RABBIT

VCCV

- To divide "rabbit," break up the word between the two consonants.
- Use colored pens to make the vowels red and the consonants blue.

RAB/BIT

V C / C V

- Now you can box the word like this:

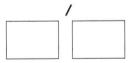

RAB	**BIT**
1st syllable	**2nd syllable**

Try this exercise again with two words of your choosing.

Word 1

_____

Word 2

_____

32. Five Types of Syllable Division: Pony

"Pony" is a V/CV word. Follow these steps to divide this word type.

● Look at the word "pony." Under the word, mark the letters as vowels (V) or consonants (C). Start at the first vowel.

PONY

_____

● Keep marking until you meet another vowel, then stop. Only mark vowel to vowel.
● To divide "pony," break up the word after the first vowel.
● Use colored pens to make the vowels red and the consonants blue.

PO/NY

V/CV

● Now you can box the word like this:

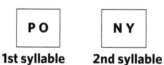

PO	NY
1st syllable	**2nd syllable**

Repeat the process for these words, and then for two of your own.

RAVEN

_____

ZERO

_____

Your word: _____

_____

Your word: _____

_____

Tips

Remember to begin with the first vowel and keep marking consonants until you arrive at the next vowel. And don't forget! Y is a vowel if it comes at the end of a word.

33. **Five Types of Syllable Division: Robin**

"Robin" is a VC/V word. Follow these steps to divide this word type.

- Look at the word "robin." Under the word, mark the letters as vowels (V) or consonants (C). Start at the first vowel.

ROBIN

_____

- Keep marking until you meet another vowel, then stop. Only mark vowel to vowel.
- To divide "robin," split the word after the first consonant that follows the vowel.
- Use colored pens to make the vowels red and the consonants blue.

ROB/IN

VC/V

- Now you can box the word like this:

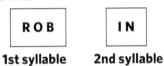

ROB	IN
1st syllable	**2nd syllable**

Repeat the process for these words, and then for two of your own.

RAPID

_____

TONIC

_____

Your word: _____

_____

Your word: _____

_____

34. Five Types of Syllable Division: Monster

"Monster" is an example of a VC/CCV word. Follow these steps to divide this word type.

- Look at the word "monster." Under the word, mark the letters as vowels (V) or consonants (C). Start at the first vowel.

MONSTER

_____

- Keep marking until you meet another vowel, then stop. Only mark vowel to vowel.
- To divide "monster," break up the word between the three consonants that follow the vowel. But watch out! You need to keep the ST blend together.
- Now, use colored pens to make the vowels red and the consonants blue.

MONSTER

V C / C C V

- Now you can box the word like this:

MON	STER
1st syllable	**2nd syllable**

Repeat the process for these words, and then for two of your own.

BATHTUB

_____

PUMPKIN

_____

Your word: _____

_____

Your word: _____

_____

35. **Five Types of Syllable Division: Lion**

"Lion" is a CV/VC word. Follow these steps to divide this word type.

- Look at the word "lion." Under the word, mark the letters as vowels (V) or consonants (C).

L I O N

———————

- Keep marking until you meet another vowel, then stop. Only mark vowel to vowel. (Don't worry about marking the last consonant.)
- To divide "lion," break up the word between the two vowels.
- Now, use colored pens to make the vowels red and the consonants blue.

L I / O N

<u>C V / V</u>

- Now you can box the word like this:

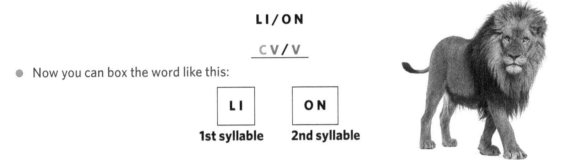

L I	O N
1st syllable	**2nd syllable**

Repeat the process for these words, and then for two of your own.

FUEL

_____

CREATE

_____

Your word: _____

_____

Your word: _____

_____

Watch Out!

When two vowels are next to each other but do not work as a team, the word will divide like "lion" (e.g., di/et), but if the two vowels work as a team, as in "boat," the word will be one syllable.

30. Multisyllabic Mastery

This activity uses the names of people and teams to help you practice syllable division. Some of the names have multiple syllables and different types of syllables.

First, fill in the team for each player. Then, for each player's last name and for each team's name, mark where the syllables break or divide. For example, for Jaylen Brown, you would divide "Brown" and "Celtics." (Note: "Brown" is one syllable because it only has one vowel sound.)

Name of Player	Team	Name of Player	Team
Jaylen Brown	Cel/tics	Anthony Davis	Lak/ers
Gordon Hayward		LeBron James	
Marcus Smart		Dwight Howard	
Jayson Tatum		Kyle Kuzma	
Kemba Walker		JaVale McGee	
Kevin Durant	Nets	Jimmy Butler	Heat
Kyrie Irving		Bam Adebayo	
Joe Harris		Khris Middleton	Bucks
Klay Thompson		Devon Booker	Suns
Stephen Curry		Damian Lillard	Trail Blazers
James Harden	Nets	Harrison Barnes	Kings
Russell Westbrook		DeMar DeRozan	Spurs
Malcolm Brogdon	Pacers	LaMarcus Aldridge	
Victor Oladipo		Derrick White	
Myles Turner		Kyle Lowry	Raptors

37. **Syllable Types**

Earlier in this section, we looked at six types of syllables: closed syllables, open syllables, consonant + LE syllables, vowel/consonant/E syllables, R-controlled syllables, and vowel team syllables.

   This activity will practice noticing syllable patterns. Write a name from the Players List in the appropriate box in the chart below, marking to denote the syllable type. For the consonant + LE syllable type, come up with a fake name that fits using the correct pattern. If any player has more than one syllable type, put them in more than one category.

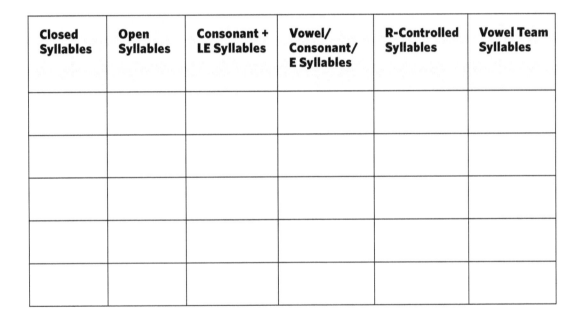

Closed Syllables	Open Syllables	Consonant + LE Syllables	Vowel/ Consonant/ E Syllables	R-Controlled Syllables	Vowel Team Syllables

Players List

White	Turner	Brown	Brogdon
Booker	Oladipo	Beal	Green
Davis	Walker	Tatum	Drummond
James	Lopez	Harris	Butler
Joe	Plumlee	Mike	Love

38. Rules and Tips for Dividing Syllables

These are quick tips for syllable division. Making up your own examples is a good way to remember these syllable patterns. There is one example for each type in the chart, so think of two more examples for each syllable type in the space provided.

Syllables	Example	Example	Example
Between two consonants	tur/nip		
Usually after first vowel	de/pend		
Between compound words	work/out		
Between vowels if they make separate sounds	di/et		
Before consonant + LE	ket/tle		

39. **Take the Pop Quiz!**

1. Complete this sentence: Every word must contain a syllable with a _____

_____.

2. How many syllables do you hear in this nonsense word: "yogonda"?

3. A vowel team syllable is when _____ to make one _____.

4. A closed syllable is when the vowel is _____ as in the word _____.

5. Why is the R-controlled syllable called the Bossy R? Give an example word that contains the Bossy R. _____

6. Using the information on syllable division, give an example of a word for each of these syllable types.

    a. VC/CV _____

    b. V/CV _____

    c. VC/V _____

    d. VC/CCV or VCC/CV _____

    e. CV/VC _____

7. Which word is an example of a consonant + LE syllable word?

    a. jam

    b. butter

    c. table

    d. travel

8. The word "tiger" has a _____ syllable at the end of the first syllable.

    a. closed

    b. open

    c. R-controlled

    d. vowel team

➡

9. Give an example of a word that can be described as multisyllabic (more than one sylla-ble) and indicate how many syllables are in the word. _____

10. Write your full name and label each type of syllable in your name.

For example, my name is Gavin Reid. "Gavin" is made up of closed syllables because each syllable has short vowels protected by a consonant. My last name is a vowel team syllable because EI in "Reid" makes only one sound.

_____

Tips and Tools

Sometimes we can become overwhelmed by the amount of information on a topic. We might start by using the Internet or reading some books to find out more about the topic. But there's often too much information for us to read and understand, which can make us feel that the task is impossible.

When this happens, make a chart like the one below. It helps to think of what you already know, and at the end, you can write short, key points.

WHAT I ALREADY KNOW	WHAT DO I HAVE TO FIND OUT?	WHERE WILL I OBTAIN THE INFORMATION?	KEY POINTS

Prefixes, Suffixes, Base Words, and Root Words

40. Word Sort

Base words are whole words that stand alone and cannot be broken down into smaller parts. They give meaning to the word. Prefixes and suffixes can be added to base words to change the meaning.

A prefix is a unit of meaning added to the beginning of a word.
A suffix is a unit of meaning added to the end of a word.

It's important to be able to recognize prefixes, suffixes, and base words. Look at the following words and determine if there is a prefix or a suffix in the word. The first two rows have been done as examples.

Word	Base Word	Prefix	Suffix
happiness	happy		NESS
displace	place	DIS	
sociable			
games			
joyful			
cupful			
matted			
lovely			
doing			
undo			
covering			
uncover			

41. **Back to Base Words**

A base word is a word that can stand on its own. A prefix or a suffix can be added to change the meaning of the word. Prefixes can even change the meaning to the opposite of the base word.

This is an activity to practice spotting base words. Look at the following words. If it's a base word, write it in the second column. If it is a word with a prefix or suffix, write it in the third column and write which one it has (prefix or suffix).

Word	Base Words	Words with a Prefix or Suffix
impossible		impossible (prefix)
do	do	
read		
restless		
debunk		
pack		
deck		
friend		
dismiss		
replay		
run		
berries		
cart		
trapped		

42. Preparing for Prefixes

Prefixes are important because they can change the meaning of a word. A prefix is a unit of meaning (a small group of words) placed before another word.

Draw a line between a base word and a prefix to make a new word. Write the words on the lines next to the chart. The first one is completed as an example. Please note, the base word doesn't necessarily match with the prefix next to it, and there may be more than one correct prefix that can be added to make a word!

Prefix		Base Word	
de		pend	depend
un		take	
dis		perfect	
pre		done	
mis		tour	
re		to	
de		possible	
over		cue	
in		just	
mis		camp	
im		happy	
dis		cue	
im		amble	
semi		play	

43. Prefixes Change the Meaning

Prefixes change the meaning of the base word. For example, the prefix pre- means "before," and the prefix mis- means "wrongly." In this exercise, write the meaning of the base word and then write the meaning of the base word with the prefix to show how the prefix changed the meaning.

Word	Meaning	With Prefix	Meaning
light	something bright	delight	a state of happiness
vent		prevent	
come		become	
act		overact	
act		react	
equal		unequal	
appear		reappear	
appear		disappear	
side		beside	
sense		nonsense	
place		misplace	
do		undo	
visible		invisible	
fix		prefix	

44. Suffixes: You Can Do It!

A suffix can also change the meaning of the base word. It can add further meaning to a word and give it more importance. A suffix can also change the part of speech of the word. For example, the word "quick" can become "quickly" by adding the suffix LY.

For this activity, add suffixes to the base words, then write the meaning of the new word in the third column. The first example is done for you.

Word	With Suffix	Meaning
music (noun)	musical (adjective)	good at music
music	musician	
jump	jumpy	
skip	skipper	
hand	handful	
spot	spotless	
home	homeless	
mad	madly	
in	inward	
hope	hopeful	
inform	informative	

45. Understanding Prefixes and Suffixes

This activity focuses on the meaning of words that have prefixes and suffixes.

In this activity, you will complete the sentence below for each word pair from the word bank. Be sure to circle the word from the word pair you want to write about first.

**I would rather (be) _____ [using one of the option words] because_____
[say why].**

For example:

Would you rather be *thoughtful / thoughtless*?

**I would rather be <u>thoughtful</u> because <u>it is more rewarding and I like to make</u>
<u>people happy</u>.**

1. I would rather (be) _____ because _____.

2. I would rather (be) _____ because _____.

3. I would rather (be) _____ because _____.

4. I would rather (be) _____ because _____.

5. I would rather (be) _____ because _____.

6. I would rather (be) _____ because _____.

7. I would rather (be) _____ because _____.

8. I would rather (be) _____ because _____.

9. I would rather (be) _____ because _____.

10. I would rather (be) _____ because _____.

helpless / helpful	**produce / deduce**
inactive / proactive	**dispel / propel**
insensitive / sensitive	**preserve / serve**
unpleasant / pleasant	**perfect / defect**
disappear / reappear	**affected / unaffected**

46. Circle for Success

Practice recognizing the correct meaning of a word with a prefix or suffix. First, read the paragraph below. Then, circle the word from the word pair that best fits the sentence.

Music Magic

Streamed / *Streaming* music is a way of playing music. It's playing music directly

inline / *online* in *unreal-time* / *real-time* without having to *download* / *downsize* it

first. It has been the *response* / *responsibility* that *principal* / *principality* music /

musical labels and *outlets* / *inlets* have found brings in *outcome* / *income.*

Presently / *Present* you can *access* / *accessible* all available music, as much as you

want, *whenever* / *however* you want. If you have an *insatiable* / *satiable* appetite

for music, this lets you *obtain* / *detain* as much music as you want.

47. **Rest and Relax**

ER is a very common suffix. Some words using this suffix become different parts of speech. For example, the verb "compute" can become the noun "computer," and the verb "clean" can become the adjective "cleaner." This exercise will focus on when to use ER suffixes. It will also help you review the grammatical parts of speech.

Describe your ideal room. As you write, include five things you want in your room (nouns with ER suffix) and five words to describe your room (adjectives with ER suffix). You don't have to write what your room really looks like. You can make it up so you are able to use these words!

Here are some words to get you started:

computer	cleaner	tidier
recorder	printer	record player
transformer	scanner	poster
clutter	quieter	noisier
glitter	bigger	taller

My Relaxation Place

_____

_____

_____

_____

_____

_____

_____

40. Base Word Families

This activity is about base word families. Family words are the different kinds of words that can be made from a base word by using a prefix or suffix. Practicing with base word families will extend your vocabulary knowledge and help with written work.

For this activity, write a base word in the first column of the following table. In the next three columns, add a prefix or a suffix to the base word to create a family word. Three rows are already completed for you.

Base Word	Family Word	Family Word	Family Word
transport	transportation	transportable	transported
solve	dissolve	solution	solvable

When the table is completed, create a diagram like this one on a separate sheet of paper to show the word family connections.

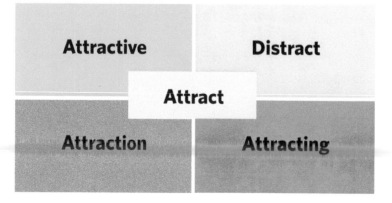

49. **Final E Spelling Rule**

There are only six spelling rules that you need to know in order to be a successful speller. The Final E spelling rule is one of the easiest to remember. Here are the steps to follow in the Final E Rule:

1. Locate the base word and the suffix in the word. Remember, you will find the suffix at the end of the word.

2. Determine if the base word ends with an E. (Note that this rule applies mostly to words that have the vowel/consonant/E syllable type.)

3. Now, look at the suffix. If the suffix begins with a vowel, you will drop the E on the base word. For example, "hope + ing." The base word "hope" has an E at the end. The suffix ING starts with a vowel, so you drop the E from "hope" and spell your new word "hoping."

4. If the suffix starts with a consonant, you will keep the E. Using the same base word "hope" with the suffix FUL, the word would be "hope + ful." The word "hope" ends with an E, but the suffix FUL starts with a consonant, so we would keep the E. You would spell your new word "hopeful."

   Look at the words with suffixes below. Decide if you need to drop, or keep, the final E for each one. Write out what the word is. Then, write that same word around its appropriate image—a trash can for "tossing" the final E, or a piggy bank for saving it!

hope + ful = _____   **chase + ing =** _____

drive + ing = _____   **grace + less =** _____

bake + ed = _____   **broke + en =** _____

shake + able = _____   **bride + s =** _____

Drop the E   Keep the E

50. Double or Nothing

The 1.1.1 Doubling Rule is another spelling rule, and it's easy to follow. A word must have one syllable, one short vowel, and only one final consonant to follow this rule. Also, the suffix must start with a vowel. If the word has all of these, then the final consonant of the base word is doubled before adding the suffix.

For example, "sitting" has two Ts because the base word, "sit," has one syllable, a short vowel, one final consonant, and the suffix starts with an I. "Eating," however, has one T. Why? Because the E in the base word, "eat," is long. Be aware that the letter X never doubles even if the word follows the 1.1.1 Doubling Rule.

Use the chart below to decide if you double the final consonant of the base word before adding the suffix. Look at the word and the column headings. Draw an emoji in each of the boxes that describe the word. If you have emojis in all of the boxes, then double the final consonant. The first one is done for you.

Base Word	Suffix	One Syllable	Short Vowel	One Final Consonant	Suffix Starts with a Vowel	Word
sit	ing	😊	😐	😖	😮	sitting
grab	ed					
grow	ing					
kick	ing					
stream	ing					
seat	ed					
eat	ing					

51. Spelling: Final Y Rule and Word Search

It is important to know when to keep or change the Y at the end of a word when adding a suffix. **When a word ends with Y and there is a consonant before it, change the Y to I and add your suffix.**

For this activity you will decide if the Y stays or if it changes to an I. Write the word with the correct spelling in the bottom box. One has already been done for you. Then, try to find those same words in the word search.

j	o	y	f	u	l	e	n	t	t	l
e	s	i	e	t	r	e	i	s	a	e
n	p	d	j	t	e	s	e	e	u	j
d	c	e	r	s	p	i	t	o	r	t
o	t	y	p	e	n	e	e	e	d	o
s	s	e	n	i	p	p	a	h	e	y
i	u	v	t	t	t	l	e	i	n	i
p	p	n	e	t	g	i	i	i	i	n
p	r	o	i	e	f	i	f	e	e	g
c	i	c	y	r	d	e	s	u	d	t
s	n	t	t	p	e	d	o	o	l	y

joy + ful =
pity + ful =
toy + ing = toying
deny + ed =
reply + ed =
easy + er =
tiny + est =
pretty + est =
happy + ness =
convey + ed =

52. Know Your Roots

Knowing where language comes from is important for reading and spelling. English has been influenced and formed by many different languages. Many English words contain affixes from the Latin and Greek languages.

Latin affixes: Subjects such as literature and the social sciences use words with Latin affixes, like the suffix TION. Some common letter combinations you will find in Latin roots include CT and PT. Latin affixes don't usually contain vowel digraphs. Many Latin-based words are made by combining a prefix with a root and a suffix.

Greek affixes: Many of these types of affixes can be found in the sciences and in medical words. Just like Latin, Greek affixes can be identified by certain letter combinations. Some common combinations include PH, CH (pronounced /k/), silent P (such as PS, PT, and PN), RH, MN, and a Y that sounds like a short I.

For this activity, put the words from the box in the appropriate column. Then, underline the part of the word that helped you discover the origin.

phonology chemistry phonograph bankrupt
psychology connection abruptly ejected gym collected
eruption dictate interruption prescription

Greek   **Latin**

_____   _____

_____   _____

_____   _____

_____   _____

_____   _____

_____   _____

53. Suffixes: More Than Just an Ending

Many suffixes indicate a certain part of speech. Here are some of the most common ways to categorize suffixes:

Noun Suffixes	Adjective Suffixes	Verb Suffixes	Adverb Suffixes
TION (subtraction)	FUL (graceful)	ED (jumped)	LY (carefully)
ING (icing)	LESS (harmless)	ING (chewing)	
S (dogs)	ING (interesting)	S (plays)	
ISM (communism)	ED (excited)		
NESS (kindness)	ER (bigger)		
MENT (achievement)	EST (biggest)		

Use the words from the table above to fill in the blanks in the sentences below. Try to decide if the word is a verb, noun, or adjective. Circle the part of speech at the end of the sentence.

Hint: Look at the sentence and decide the purpose of the word. Usually, nouns come at the beginning of a sentence and verbs come second. Adjectives describe nouns and often come in front of them. For example, in "interesting newspaper," "newspaper" is the noun. "Interesting" comes before the noun and describes it, so "interesting" is an adjective.

1. The _____ dancer was also very beautiful. (adjective / verb)

2. The _____ driver could not stop honking his horn. (verb / adjective)

3. It was an extremely _____ newspaper article. (adjective / verb)

4. He _____ all day long for his favorite TV program. (verb / noun)

5. The traffic light _____ colors while he changed radio stations. (verb / noun)

6. _____ is full of lots of sugar. (verb / noun)

7. _____ is the act of taking one number away from another number. (noun / adjective)

8. The _____ were false and misleading. (noun / adjective)

9. He thought he had made the _____ mistake of his life! (adjective / verb)

10. The _____ repetition of the activity brought tears to his eyes. (noun / adjective)

54. Detective Work 101

Suffixes are important in vocabulary, and so are prefixes! Sometimes you might not recognize prefixes when you're reading and studying. Other times, you might see prefixes related to words that you already know. You would be surprised by how much you actually already know!

Read the words in the word bank below and try to match the prefix with its meaning. Use the clues contained within the words to figure out the meaning of the prefix. Then, fill in the blanks in each box with your own words that use the same prefix.

reprinted
resend
redo
reread
rethread
rewrite
_____
_____

Meaning of RE:

subway
submarine
submerge
subtitle
subheading
_____
_____

Meaning of SUB:

preorder
preset
preheat
prepay
prepurchase
precook
_____
_____

Meaning of PRE:

unlock
unfinished
unread
unclean
unrest
unfolded
unpack
_____
_____

Meaning of UN:

below or under / to do again / before / wrong or bad

55. **Rainbow Corners**

Now that you are an expert at prefixes, roots, and suffixes, try making some words on your own.

   Using at least 12 different colored pencils, crayons, or markers, connect prefixes from box 1 to roots in box 2, then to suffixes in box 3. In box 4, write the new word you have created on each line. You must work clockwise going from box 1 to box 2 to box 3 to box 4. Make sure you create real words. If you are unsure, use a dictionary. Remember your spelling rules as you write your new word on the line. You might have to drop or double some letters to create a word! You may use prefixes, roots, or suffixes multiple times to create words.

1	2
RE PRE MIS IN PRO	send SECT RUPT help read
UN DIS TRANS DE DIS	JECT SPECT GRAM phone graph
BI TRI DI CON SUB	hope part script scope act print
PRO TRANS BIO MICRO	lock hope think TRACT head spell
POST OVER	heat scope MERGE angle

4	3
<u>unlocked</u> _____ _____ _____ _____ _____ _____	FUL LESS ITY Y ED ING ER EST ABLE IC ENT ISM IST IFY ISH IVE IZE NESS LY MENT OUS SHIP Y

56. Kicking Rules!

There were three spelling rules in this chapter: the 1.1.1 Doubling Rule, the Final E Rule, and the Final Y Rule. In this activity, you'll review and practice identifying words that use these rules.

Look at the word list below. "Kick" the word into the appropriate goal according to which rule it follows. Do this by drawing a line from the ball to the net.

1.1.1 Doubling Rule   **Final E Rule**   **Final Y Rule**

dotting

denied

striving

replacing

braver

spotting

replied

cried

swimming

fried

butted

craved

removing

batting

complied

stored

making

likable

dubbed

funny

piping

skating

reserving

adorable

letting

wetting

biggest

copied

craziest

having

57. List It!

Prefixes, suffixes, and roots are everywhere. Many times, we don't realize how much we know. Try this game called List It, and you will be surprised by how many prefixes and suffixes you already know!

For this exercise, roll a die and follow the instructions on the square. Challenge yourself to improve your knowledge of affixes!

List 5 words with the prefix PRE	List 6 words with the root PORT	List 6 prefixes that you know	List 5 words with the suffix ING	List 5 words with the suffix EST
List 5 words with the prefix RE	List 3 words with the prefix SUB	List 3 words with the suffix ED	List 5 words with the prefix UN	List 3 words with the suffix SHIP
List 4 words with the root STRUCT	List 5 roots that you know	List 5 suffixes that you know	List 4 roots that are Latin based	List the suffix that means "more than" or "someone who"
List 5 prefixes you would find in your science book	List 4 prefixes from Greek origins	List 3 prefixes or suffixes related to weather	List your favorite suffix	List 6 prefixes related to mathematics
List 5 words with the root TRACT	List your favorite prefix	List 3 prefixes related to outer space	List 2 words with the prefix EX	List 5 prefixes that mean "opposite" or "not"

58. Roll and Build

Practicing word building helps you improve your vocabulary and be a better word detective. Noticing how words are constructed will build your skills in spelling and writing.

Roll a die, then build a word using the prefixes, suffixes, and roots listed in the chart that match the number on your die. Write the words at the bottom of the page. Practice this alone or challenge a friend or a family member to improve their skills as well! Prefixes are in green, suffixes are in red, and roots are in black.

1	2	3	4	5	6
STRUCT	ER	ED	UN	ACT	SECT
PRE	EST	ING	LESS	OVER	TRI
NESS	RE	TRACT	FUL	UNDER	SPECT
BIO	TRANS	SPECT	Y	FREE	MIS
EX	FORM	PRO	ION	ISM	MID
S	STRUCT	BI	DE	IST	TRANS

_____

_____

_____

_____

_____

_____

59. **Take the Pop Quiz!**

Time for a quick review!

1. What is a suffix? _____

2. What is a prefix? _____

3. What is a root? _____

4. What does the 1.1.1 Doubling Rule tell us to do?

   a. Double the word.

   b. Drop the suffix.

   c. Double the final consonant if the word has one syllable, one short vowel, and one final consonant, and the suffix starts with a vowel.

5. Where do 80 percent of English words come from?

   a. Latin

   b. Greek

   c. French

6. What letter needs to be before a Y in order for the Y to change into an I?

   a. a consonant

   b. a vowel

7. A _____ comes at the end of a word.

   a. suffix

   b. root

   c. prefix

8. Where do you find a root?

   a. at the end of a word

   b. in your garden

   c. in the middle of a word

➡

9. When do you drop the E in the Final E spelling rule?

    a. when the suffix starts with a consonant

    b. when the suffix starts with a vowel

10. What does the prefix RE mean?

    a. to do again

    b. not or opposite

    c. someone who

Tips and Tools

Note-taking can be very difficult. Sometimes students will take too many notes or copy whole chunks from a book without really understanding them. Note-taking can be more effective if you have a system.

    If you are taking notes from a book, here are some tips to consider:

- Look at the contents page and the index first. Familiarize yourself with these and jot down the chapters or pages from the index that you think are important.

- Think of the questions you want answered from this book. Jot down some questions. Use the words "what," "why," "where," and "who." You may not use all of the question words, but some of them might be useful.

- Glance through the chapters you have highlighted and note some key points. Try to keep your key points to around four words.

- Reread and write down evidence to support your key points.

- Try to discuss these points with a friend!

Word Recognition

60. Word Recognition and Sight Words

So far, this book has focused on words that follow some kind of pattern, but there are many words in the English language that do not fit into a pattern. These are called sight words. They have to be remembered in other ways. Sight words tend to be very common words and difficult to sound out, so it's important to memorize them.

For this exercise, complete the sentence or phrase with a sight word from the list.

It's a good idea to take your time reading these words the first time around. After a few practices, try to speed up. Set a target time to beat!

Sight Words

where	who	said	pretty
there	often	busy	island
from	through	which	
people	enough	beautiful	

1. "_____ are you?" asked the ghost.

2. I am _____ Canada.

3. "_____ has the class gone to?" asked the teacher.

4. Please stand over _____ after your photo has been taken.

5. The crowd was full of _____ from around the world.

6. The dog ran _____ the open door and into the kitchen for his dinner.

7. "I can never get _____ chocolate!" replied the young girl.

8. My mom _____ to take this to this note to the teacher and make sure she reads it.

9. I _____ eat white chocolate. I never eat milk or dark chocolate.

10. These days, I'm very _____ at school with lots of extra projects and homework.

11. _____ picture do you prefer?

12. The freshly planted garden looked _____ in the late afternoon sun.

13. The young girl looked extremely _____ in her new outfit.

14. Most people don't know it, but England is an _____.

61. **Writing with Sight Words**

Make your own 10 sentences from these words. Try to include at least two sight words in each sentence.

Words

two	what	one	who
could	do	were	because
from	was	very	said
only	busy	friend	there
they	people	pretty	beautiful
island	give	live	iron
are	only	another	through
would	month	rough	here
tough	where	have	February
your	should	enough	which

My 10 Sentences:

1. _____

2. _____

3. _____

4. _____

5. _____

6. _____

7. _____

8. _____

9. _____

10. _____

62. Nonsense or Not ✔

In the English language, some combinations of letters will never appear next to each other. For example, you will not find DGE at the beginning of an English word. In this activity, practice spotting real words and nonsense words, sometimes called nonwords or pseudo-words (meaning made-up words).

Circle the real words. Those that are not circled will be nonwords.

table	jqin	baqg	draw
srheld	iqak	bring	vgical
laugh	warm	vpes	done
qyed	bird	bten	qken
avwze	corn	zhel	eye

63. Sight Word Hunt

You are on a field trip with your friends at school, and you need to spot all the sight words on your trip. The first few sentences are written for you, and the sight words are underlined. Finish the story by including and underlining more sight words.

Downtown Celebration

We **were** excited about **the** trip to downtown. We had been downtown before but not for **such** an important occasion as this. Our basketball team **was** coming home with **the** trophy. Seeing state champions is quite an honor! The streets and **the** sidewalks **were** crammed with **people.**

_____

_____

_____

_____

_____

_____

64. **Word Within a Word**

Being able to find shorter or smaller words within a longer word helps you read and identify words quickly. This activity is practice for finding smaller words within a bigger word. See how many smaller words you can discover or make with the letters in each word. An example has been done for you. Use a dictionary if you aren't sure of any words. Have fun!

establishment

tab   test

bliss   name

ten   hate

stab   men

able   haste

combination

_____

_____

embarrassment

_____

_____

hypothyroidism

_____

_____

geographical

_____

_____

spectator

_____

_____

65. **Unpacking Words**

Being able to identify word parts such as prefixes, suffixes, or root words (skills learned in the previous section) helps you quickly recognize or decode a word. When you can quickly find the parts in a word and break the word into smaller chunks, you can read it faster.

Take a look at the following words. Unpack the prefixes in one suitcase, the suffixes in a different suitcase, and the roots or base words in another suitcase. After you have done this, read each unit separately and then blend them together again. After breaking apart and blending the words back together, read the words again and time yourself to see how quickly you can read them. Be careful! Some of the words might be missing letters because of spelling rules, and some words may have more than one suffix. An example has been done for you.

Example: precooked

pre

cook

ed

misplaced	unlocked	important	repacking
resending	inserting	containment	excluding
unfocused	unfinished	reaction	playfulness

66. Sight Word Sort

You'll encounter many types of words while you read. Some may be decodable, which means that you can sound them out. Another type of word you may encounter is a sight word. Sight words need to be memorized because they do not follow traditional rules. Their letter patterns are rare, so they are difficult to sound out. Sight words make up a small percentage of words in the English language, but they often cause the most amount of stress because you need practice recognizing them. A good way to spot sight words is to ask yourself a couple of questions:

Is the word pronounced the way that it is spelled?

Does the letter pattern follow a pattern commonly found in English?

Are there any letters that are not pronounced or skipped over?

Do the vowels say their traditional short or long sound?

Sort the following list of words into two categories, sight words and non-sight words. Place the sight words under the picture of the binoculars and the words you can sound out under the music note.

have	said	they	made	friend	Wednesday
glad	drinking	what	were	at	him
we	helping	give	people	nest	eating
spoon	because	once	who	she	her

67. Create Your Own Mnemonic

Sight words (those tricky words that need to be memorized) can be difficult not only to read, but also to spell, because they don't follow the rules. One way to help you remember how to spell sight words is to create a memory trick called a mnemonic. A mnemonic can be a short sentence that reminds you how to spell a word. For example, a mnemonic for the word "because" might be: "Big Elephants Can Actually Understand Small Elephants." The first letter of each word in this saying corresponds with the letters in the word "because." It's a trick to make spelling easier.

Create a mnemonic for these popular sight words and then draw a picture that corresponds with the mnemonic you created. Use the example from above to help you create your own mnemonic.

Word	Mnemonic	Picture
America		
their		
once		
sound		
answer		
people		
Wednesday		
January		

68. Music While You Learn

Music can have many different functions. It can help you relax and make you feel good. It can give you someone to identify with, if you are a big fan of the artist. Music can also help you learn. It can be like an extra teacher. Let's use it to practice spelling.

In this activity, first say the sight word, then tap, sing, jump, and do push-ups while spelling the word. Then, find a word that rhymes and use the word in a sentence. Here are words to get you started.

build	**business**
because	**pretty**
friend	**beautiful**

Actions to Help You Learn	
1. Say it	
2. Tap it	
3. Sing it	
4. Jump to it	
5. Do push-ups	
6. Rhyme it	said... bed
7. Use it	

69. **One for All**

Knowing word families can help with reading and spelling. Word families are groups of words that have a common group of letters, such as IGHT, INK, ING, and ALL. Once you recognize the pattern, you can read lots of words with the same pattern. For example, if you know the pattern IGHT, you can read "light," "night," and "sight" more easily.

Complete the table with other words from the same word family. Two examples are done for each family. Complete eight more for each family.

IGHT	INK	ING	ALL	ION
sight	pink	ping	fall	station
night	link	sing	tall	stallion

More practice: Make a set of word family playing cards using all 50 words in the table above. Write a different word on each card and shuffle the pack. Divide the pack with the other players (two to four players) and play Snap. You can also play a board game with dice and use the cards as markers in each space. The winner is the person who collects the most word families (a set of three will count as one set of a word family).

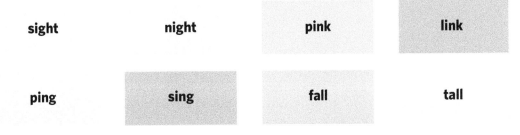

70. Earth, Sea, and Sky

Over 80 percent of English words are borrowed from Latin, and it is estimated that over 150,000 English words come from Greek. Knowing the roots of language can help you build longer and more elaborate words. For example, the Greek word "micro" means "small," and some English words are derived (or taken) from "micro"—for example, "microscope." As a general rule, words that begin with PH, like "physical," are usually of Greek origin.

Knowing the roots of words can help with word recognition and spelling. Here are some examples for earth, sea, and sky:

Earth: GEO (Greek) as in "geography." Also TERRA (Latin), as in "terrain."

Sea: MAR (Latin) as in "marina." (Some ancient Greek words, including Aphrodite, Atlantis, and Poseidon, also refer to the sea. A Latin example is Neptune.)

Sky: ASTRO (Greek) as in "astronomy," "planet" from the Greek word for "wanderer," and "luna" (Latin), which means moon, hence the word "lunar."

Using the topics of earth, sea, and sky, write words with Greek or Latin origins in the boxes below.

Clues

- Earth: Think about mountain ranges, vegetation, and land features.
- Sea: Think about words with MAR or words related to sea gods.
- Sky: Think about planets and words related to flying or the sun (e.g., SOL).

Write examples in the boxes below.

71. Using Math for Word Recognition

Etymology refers to the origins of words. Knowing the origins of words can help with the special terms math, science and other subjects use (see Exercise 72 on page 78 for examples).

This activity focuses on math words and Latin prefixes relating to numbers. Look at the Latin prefixes and the meaning of the prefix, then write other words with the same prefix that are used in math or connected to numbers. One example is already done for you.

Latin Word	Meaning	Other Words
UNI	1	
BI	2	
TRI	3	
QUAD	4	quadrilateral, quadrangle, quadrant, quadruped
PENTA	5	
SEX	6	
SEPT	7	
OCT	8	
NOVEM	9	
DECEM	10	
UNDEC	11	
DUODEC	12	

Use these common Latin suffixes with the common prefixes (UNI, BI, TRI) to help create more math words:

- mathematical bases: AL
- adjectives of relation: NARY
- groups of musicians: TET
- words for multiples of something: UPLE
- number of years between two events: ENNIAL
- number of sides of something: LATERAL
- words for large numbers/ exponents: ILLION

72. **Tricky Words**

This activity is about recognizing and retaining words you might find in different subjects.

Some subject vocabulary in high school can be challenging. It can take a lot of time and practice to be able to read and understand them automatically.

Before starting this activity, look over the example chart. Some words (like "pharaoh") do not fit a regular pattern, so they have to be remembered by sight. Knowledge of Greek and Latin roots will help, too.

History	Geography	Chemistry	Biology
agricultural	latitude	chemical	physiological
industrial	longitude	chloride	protein
democracy	hemispheres	organic	chromosome
monarch	climate	potassium	cortex
revolution	environment	hydrogen	epidermis
English	**Mathematics**	**Art**	**Physical Education**
metaphor	calculate	sculpture	substitute
syntax	equation	photography	referee
poetic	symbol	texture	spectator
dramatic	angular	sketch	exercise
rhyme	symmetry	vertical	physique

In the chart below, write the subjects you want to learn. Use the words from the previous list in the second column. Then, research or look online for origins and meanings in order to fill in the last two columns.

Subject	Word	How I Will Remember It	Meaning of Word
geography	hemisphere	It is of Greek origin and is a combination of the prefix HEMI, which means "half," and SPHERE, which means "round."	Part of a two-piece entity, e.g., a brain has a left and a right hemisphere.

73. **Know Your Lane**

Word parts are always in the same position in a word (beginning, middle, or end). It is helpful to memorize where word parts are usually located in order to use them to help you read and spell faster.

Put the prefixes, suffixes, and roots/bases from the box below into the correct lane (beginning, middle, or end) Some examples have been done for you. Be careful!

TION	**ION**	**MENT**	**RE**	**ING**	**ED**	**PRE**	quick	print	**LY**	**FUL**	**LESS**
ER	**EST**	**DE**	part	**ANT**	kick	**IC**	spell	drink	trust	**STRUCT**	**S**	**ENT**
IN	**UN**	**TRACT**	like	stand	**NESS**	**ES**	bless	hope	care	play	**MIS**

Beginning	Middle	End
MIS		ENT
	stand	

74. Positional Spellings

Knowing when and where you see certain spelling choices is helpful for spelling and word recognition. At times, it can be very confusing to keep track of all the different options. Let's take a look at some common spellings and their patterns so that you can become more confident in your own spelling!

- **CK:** Always comes after a short vowel ("stack," "deck," "track")

- **K:** Comes at the beginning of a word with I, E, or Y ("kick," "kilt," "kelp") and in the middle of words with vowel/consonant/E syllables or R-controlled vowels ("bake," "strike," "stark," "stork")

- **C:** Comes at the beginning of a word with O, A, or U ("cap," "cute," "camp")

- **C:** Says its soft sound with I, E, or Y ("city," "cedar," "cyber")

- **TCH:** Comes after a short vowel and never at the beginning of a word

- **CH:** Comes at the beginning of a word or at the end after a long vowel, vowel team, or R-controlled vowel

- **DGE:** Comes after a short vowel and never at the beginning of a word

- **J:** Comes at the beginning of a word and never at the end

- **GE:** Comes at the end of a word after a long vowel, R-controlled vowel, or vowel team

Complete the spelling of each word and then categorize which runner they belong to. Do they belong at the start of the race, the middle, or the end?

he__	(DGE, J)	ki__	(CK, C)	sta__	(CK, C)	loun__	(GE, J)	star__	(CK, K)
coa__	(CH, TCH)	__ump	(DGE, J)	not__	(TCH, CH)	bla__	(CK, C)	do__	(DGE, J)
__ilt	(K,C)	__ing	(K, C)	fu__	(DGE, J)	sna__	(CK, K)	du___	(TCH, CH)
spi__e	(CK, K)	de__	(K, CK)	__amp	(K, C)	bi__e	(K, CK)	smu__	(DGE, J)
bar__	(GE, DGE)	__em	(G, J)	clo__	(CK, K)	clu___	(CH, TCH)		

75. Find the Sight Word

Reading sight words automatically helps with reading fluency. The purpose of this activity is to provide practice recognizing sight words and using them in a sentence. Fill in the blanks below with one of the following sight words. Don't worry; you can use the same word multiple times.

Sight Words									
often	enough	two	tongue	your	often	because	friend	gone	February
what	business	toward	February	again	something	said	to	two	what

1. Jake hesitated entering the school building as he was late _____.

2. An interesting feature of a frog is that it has a sticky _____.

3. The family likes to go south for vacation every _____.

4. The teacher _____ to the class, "Take out your geography books."

5. There is a saying that goes, "You can feed _____ birds with one hand."

6. She was excited as her whole family isn't able to go to the cinema very _____.

7. She shouted to her friend over the noise of the fairground, "It is _____ turn now!"

8. Jeremy rushed to find his _____, but he was too late; she had _____.

9. He had no idea _____ was going on but suspected it was a shady _____.

10. It is _____ cold in _____, but at least it is the shortest month of the year.

11. The truck driver pushed his plate away and politely told the server that he had had _____.

12. The teenagers crowded around the music store _____ Lady Gaga was about to sign some photos.

13. The school superintendent walked _____ the school bus when the driver beckoned him over.

14. The shopkeeper felt there was _____ suspicious about the _____ strangers.

15. As Yvonne walked _____ school, she was trying to remember the list of _____ she needed for the school trip.

76. **Snap It**

For this activity, take photos of words you see with suffixes, prefixes, or root words. You can take pictures of billboards, road signs, or shop signs.

For example, you may see this sign that means pedestrian crossing.

For this image, the suffix is ING.

So, you need to take a picture, write the word and then the prefix, suffix, or word root.

For this image, the suffix is ION.

Do you live near a shopping mall? A photo of that would work, too. The suffix in this image is ING.

77. **Blend a Family**

You learned about word families earlier in this section. For this activity, create as many words as you can with the families you already know.

    Create words using the combinations of word families and letters in each blender. Write the new words below. An example is shown for you. If you need help, use words from previous exercises or a dictionary.

small _____   _____

    _____   _____

    _____   _____

    _____   _____

SH	SHR	BR	ING
TH	THR	GR	ANG
C	SPR	H	ALL
BL	FL	T	IGHT
TR	GL	INK	ONK
W	DR	ANK	UNK
SM	CL	ONG	UNG

78. Reading the Signs

Now that you have had lots of practice using and identifying sight words, you should notice them all around you, in shops, on billboards, and even on road signs. You might start noticing them everywhere you go!

For this activity, look at some popular signs that use sight words. Use one sight word from the box to complete the sign. There is only one correct sight word for each sign.

only

weight

away

closed

wrong

the

limit

79. Take the Pop Quiz!

1. A sight word is not spelled or pronounced the way it sounds.

    a. true

    b. false

2. A phonetic word is one that you can sound out.

    a. true

    b. false

3. A prefix comes _____.

    a. at the beginning of a word

    b. at the end of a word

    c. in the middle of the word

4. "Said" is a sight word.

    a. true

    b. false

5. A suffix comes _____.

    a. in the middle of a word

    b. at the end of a word

    c. at the beginning of a word

6. A mnemonic is _____.

    a. a musical instrument

    b. a memory strategy

    c. a type of poem

➡

7. Identifying word families is helpful because _____.

    a. It helps you read faster

    b. it can help with spelling

    c. it can help you remember words

    d. all of the above

8. Many words in English come from Latin and Greek words.

    a. true

    b. false

9. The prefix TRI means _____.

    a. 2

    b. 4

    c. 3

10. TCH comes at the beginning of a word.

    a. true

    b. false

Fluency

80. Reading Fluency

Fluency is a very important part of reading. To read fluently, you need to be proficient in reading words so you are able to read automatically. That means you do not need to stop often to try to break a word down. Reading fluency is also important for comprehension. You will understand the text better if you are able to read it fluently.

There are three main components to reading fluency: accuracy, rate (speed), and expression. Expression includes tone of voice as well as pauses at appropriate parts, such as a new paragraph. Expression is very important and indicates whether you understand the text.

To become a faster, more accurate reader, you need to master recognizing individual sounds quickly. The following activity will help you become a faster reader by helping you practice being able to quickly identify common sounds.

For this activity, you will need a handful of colored pencils in nine different colors. Practice saying the sounds as you color them according to the key. Try this activity multiple times until your speed increases and the sounds become automatic!

CK	SH	TH	CH	TCH	DGE
X	Y	QU	CK	CH	SH
TH	DGE	TCH	QU	SH	CH
CH	CH	Y	X	QU	TCH
SH	TH	X	Y	X	SH
QU	DGE	CK	TCH	TH	Y

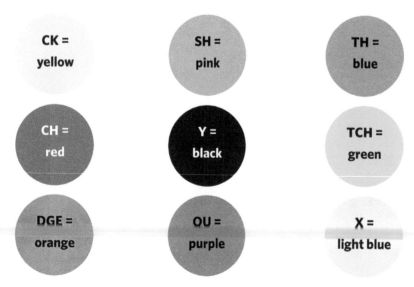

CK = yellow

SH = pink

TH = blue

CH = red

Y = black

TCH = green

DGE = orange

QU = purple

X = light blue

81. Vowels Ahead!

Vowels are important to know because every word must have one. Being able to quickly identify vowels can be very helpful.

Say the sound that each vowel team makes and then color each vowel team the appropriate color according to the key. Practice this activity many times until your speed increases and the sounds become automatic!

OA	OU	OW	ER	AI	AR
OO	EE	EA	OO	EE	AW
ER	AI	OU	OA	AR	OU
EE	ER	AW	OA	ER	EA
EA	OW	EE	AW	OO	ER
AR	AW	AI	OA	EE	EA

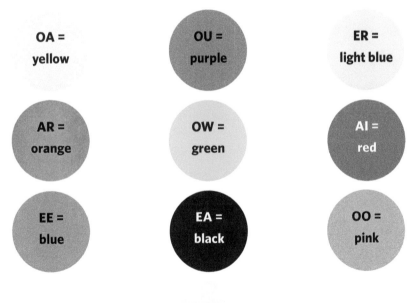

OA = yellow

OU = purple

ER = light blue

AR = orange

OW = green

AI = red

EE = blue

EA = black

OO = pink

AW = light green

82. Read the Sight Word

In the previous sections, there were activities about sight words and how to recognize them. Sight words are important to recognize because they don't always follow the rules, and trying to sound them out can slow down reading. Being able to easily identify and read sight words helps with reading fluency.

Read the sight word on the left and then circle the correct spelling of the word on the line across from the word as many times as it appears.

what	hatw	what	what	ahwt	what	ahtw	what	hwta	thaw
who	owh	who	who	how	how	hwo	who	who	ohw
said	said	aisd	dias	said	said	aisd	iads	said	dsia
two	owt	wto	two	owt	tow	tow	two	two	wot
only	only	only	only	ylon	only	only	lyon	noly	noly
very	yver	very	vyre	very	yrve	very	vrey	vrye	very
to	to	ot	to	ot	ot	to	to	ot	ot
where	hewe	where	herew	herwe	where	hrewe	where	herew	where
here	here	ereh	erhe	hrer	here	rher	rher	here	hehr
again	agian	again	again	gaina	aingn	again	again	niaig	agian

83. **Read and Roll**

There are some words in our language that are called high-frequency words. This means that they make up a large percentage of the language we use on a daily basis. Knowing how to read them quickly is helpful for your overall reading ability and fluency.

For this activity, you will need a die, a highlighter, and a timer. Set the timer for four minutes. Roll the die and read a word that corresponds to the number you have rolled. Try to finish an entire row before your time runs out. If you finish a row before the timer, you can record your best time at the bottom of the page.

him	at	and	her	home	get
go	for	jump	play	sit	but
came	ride	ran	good	have	under
want	pretty	please	say	yes	black
three	today	funny	going	green	stop

My best time: _____

84. Syllables Are Key!

Every word is made up of letter sounds and whole sound units called syllables. Every word has to have at least one syllable. Knowing about syllables helps you read longer words faster. Sounding out is a good strategy, but using larger units is more helpful.

In this activity, you'll read the key syllables and then match them up to the appropriate lock syllable. Draw a line from the key syllable to the lock syllable to make a correct word and then read the whole word quickly!

Keys	Locks
fin	ger
tar	get
win	dow
horse	shoe
ti	ger
sin	gle
re	gain
for	get
de	part
mis	place

85. Go with What You Know

When you come across a difficult word, it helps to have a "word attack strategy." Here are a couple of strategies you can use:

- First, try breaking the word down into smaller units. Does the word have a prefix? A suffix or a root you know?

- If that doesn't work, try breaking the word down into individual sounds, then sound out each sound until you get a word.

This activity has nonsense words. Circle all of the parts you know, then read the nonsense word using the smaller units. Although the words themselves are not real words, they do use real sounds, prefixes, and suffixes so that you may sound them out.

extermonting   mispleasted   pretrocked   injusted   midforsted

replocating   inkickest   unstrolding   clarting   blarted   trastion

plomping   inquestor   diverster   jimper   glostment   frofted

hilmest   clerting   examplination   recrosting

86. Sentence Slides

Reading gets easier with practice! It helps when you practice with familiar text or with shorter text that builds to longer text. Practicing passages or groups of sentences repeatedly builds fluency.

Practice reading the following sentence slides. Starting at the top, read down one line at a time. By the end of the slide, you should feel more confident in reading the words, and your reading should be faster and sound better. If you want, try timing yourself.

The
The fat
The fat chicken
The fat chicken lost
The fat chicken lost its
The fat chicken lost its wing.

The
The long
The long path
The long path will
The long path will go
The long path will go on.

Stand
Stand and
Stand and clap
Stand and clap with
Stand and clap with the
Stand and clap with the sound.

The
The drive
The drive was
The drive was long
The drive was long and
The drive was long and took forever.

The
The message
The message was
The message was hidden
The message was hidden under
The message was hidden under the table.

He
He took
He took over
He took over the
He took over the desk
He took over the desk and made a mess.

The
The wide hedge
The wide hedge was
The wide hedge was green
The wide hedge was green and cut.

Clutch
Clutch and
Clutch and grab
Clutch and grab and
Clutch and grab and hold on tight.

87. Silly Song Sentences

Who doesn't love to listen to music? Song lyrics are better when you listen carefully to the words. Songs are like poetry and can hold very special meaning. Music is almost like a universal language.

Create a silly line from a song by choosing a phrase from each device and then connecting them together to make one sentence. Practice reading the sentence, and if you like, try your hand at singing it! Don't worry if the sentences don't make sense or are a little unusual. These song lyrics can be funny.

in the middle

take a good look

at midnight

run on

seems like love

---

wait your turn

in a way

some people have

in time

at last

---

drink it up

you are the best

went too far

seems so wrong

to forget

---

boogie on down

to the beat

sending out love

kisses for you

quickly

---

but it hurts

watch you cry

in the morning

running on empty

for your love

88. Give Me a Break!

Meet our African leopard friends—Spotty and Dotty!

The box below has information about the African leopard, but unfortunately a friend texted you this information without a break or space between the words and sentences. She must have been in a hurry!

For this activity, use a colored pen to draw a line after each word. For example, "TheAfricanleopard" would be divided like this: The/African/leopard. After marking the spaces between the words, rewrite the text to make it easier to read. Think about the meaning, too. Our African leopard friends, Spotty and Dotty, will return again later in this chapter.

TheAfricanleopardcanshowagreatdealofvariationincoatcolorThisdependsonwhere itislocatedThisiscalledthehabitatThecoloroftheAfricanleopard'scoatvariesfrom apaleyellowtodeepgoldYoucanalsoseesomeblackonesMaleleopardsareusuallylarger thanfemalesSomemountainleopardsaresmallerandlessheavythanotherleopards butallleaopardsusuallyhuntatnight.

The African Leopard

_____

_____

_____

_____

_____

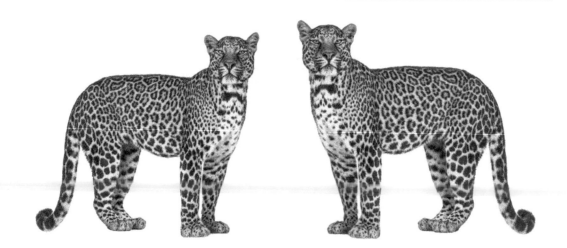

89. **Sell This Book!**

Have you ever bought a book without reading the back cover, only to be disappointed later because the book was not what you expected? Reading the reviews and synopsis on the back cover will help you pick a book you will enjoy.

Read the paragraphs on these back covers out loud and then decide which book you would purchase. Mark your preference with a dollar sign ($).

On a dark night, the quiet community neighborhood of Ravenwoods is shattered when the body of a local police officer is discovered in a building site located on the edge of the Cedargreen Forest. The neighborhood rallies for justice, but can peace be restored? Officer George H. Reid is on the case and determined to find the killer lurking in the quiet community. This unforgettable tale, with its many twists and turns, will leave you questioning the truth and who your neighbors really are.

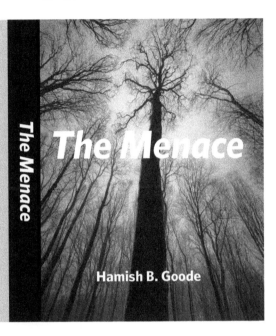

This is a heartwarming tale about two boys growing up in the country with all of the joys and turmoil of living in a remote location. Although these two best friends grow up together, they'll eventually have to choose between friendship or money. Will Joe keep the farm? Will Frank leave his hometown in hopes of pursuing his lifelong dream? The true test of friendship is at the heart of this singular story, which will leave you yearning for times past.

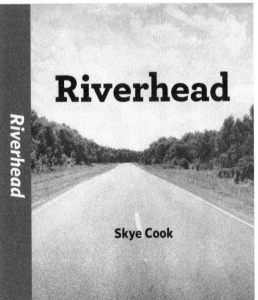

A massive snowstorm strands mountaineer Drake Firth on the top of Mount Seymour. With only a backpack and his wits, Drake is forced to decide between survival and the chance to get to the top. Does Drake have what it takes to contend with the elements, or will he give up his quest and return to the safety and comfort of civilized life? This is a riveting book about the vastness of Mother Nature and what it means to challenge yourself—a must-read for those who enjoy the great outdoors!

Sabrina Tyrell grew up with music. From the tender age of six, she sang in the church choir and became a neighborhood sensation. Rising Star is a story about a young girl's determination to make it to the top of her game, and the emotional price tag that comes with it. Gritty, real, and inspiring, this beautiful story will keep you tapping your toes and turning the pages!

90. Personal Best Reading: TV News Anchor

Reading fluency requires practice, practice, practice. These activities allow you to practice reading more fluently, accurately, and with expression. Below you will find a TV news script from Teen TV (your very own television station)!

Tonight's Anchor
Jay Jayson Jr.
Your Three-Minute News Bulletin

Read each of the following news bulletins aloud three times. Try to read them faster each time with a goal of three minutes (180 seconds) for each news bulletin.

Record your time here.

Total Time in Seconds	Tremor in Asia	Hot Cars in Tokyo	And in Sports . . .
1.			
2.			
3.			

Record your target here.

6 minutes (360 seconds) _____
5 minutes (300 seconds) _____
4 minutes (240 seconds) _____
3 minutes (180 seconds) _____
Less than 3 minutes _____

Tremor in Asia

A tremor was felt in some parts of Central Asia. It shook some tall buildings and affected a few coastal villages, but, miraculously, no serious injuries were reported. The Red Cross was on the scene very quickly as the tremor was not unexpected.

Maja, a local resident interviewed by Teen TV News, said she was hanging out some washing when she spotted a satellite dish fall from the roof of a high building close by and immediately ran for cover. She said it was terrifying as the ground under her feet started shaking.

Hot Cars in Tokyo

Tokyo's main exporter of vintage cars announced today that the new Hot Car will be launched at the May Motor Show in Minneapolis. The Hot Car comes with remote parking, a 40-inch high-definition television that can be tucked under the dashboard for easy storage, and high-powered speakers. The state-of-the-art micro engine requires just one annual service. The car only comes in ruby red, but it is sure to be a big hit with motor (and music) enthusiasts.

And in Sports . . .

Curt Johnson, soccer import from the top star-studded European team the Sparta Rangers, signed today with a mystery club in North America. No details are to be released until the deal is done and Sparta receives the $6 million fee! We spoke to a rather despondent Sparta fan today, Mr. Lee Nolak, who said, "This is surprising, but Curt will be a sensation in North America. He was our star player."

How did you do? The following exercises will help give you more practice.

91. **The Quick Sale**

Advertisements are virtually everywhere: on television, on the roadside, on transit, at rail stations, and at airports. We live in a commercial world. We are a nation of consumers, and manufacturers want us to buy their products, so advertisements are very important. They are also very expensive. Advertisement creators need to get the message across in as few words as possible, and the words need to be catchy and capture your attention.

You have to sell your mountain bike. You looked at the description online and saw some keywords you can use in your advertisement.

<table>
<tr><td align="center">mountain bike</td><td align="center">stable</td></tr>
<tr><td align="center">time trialing</td><td align="center">comfort</td></tr>
<tr><td align="center">specifically designed</td><td align="center">safety</td></tr>
<tr><td align="center">all-terrain</td><td align="center">front and rear suspension</td></tr>
<tr><td align="center">aerodynamic</td><td align="center">all colors</td></tr>
</table>

Now try to write an advertisement to sell your mountain bike. After you've written it, read it as if it will be a commercial on TV. Commercials are expensive, so you can only afford to buy 30 seconds of time.

My Advertisement: First Draft

_____

_____

_____

_____

Time how long it takes you to read your advertisement. Then, write a second draft to get your time down. If you can read that draft in less than 30 seconds, you'll be rich!

92. Would You Rather?

This activity is a fun way to practice fluency and discover some interesting choices you might make. You may discover something about yourself that you never knew before.

Read the following questions with a friend or family member and answer them. The person with the silliest answer or the most unusual answer wins—you decide!

Would you rather be tall or short?	Would you rather dance or listen to music?	Would you rather be a penguin or an elephant?	Would you rather have an electric bike or an electric car?	Would you rather be popular or a computer genius?
Would you rather be a rock star or a movie star?	Would you rather skip English class or math class?	Would you rather play soccer or hockey?	Would you rather be a Saturday or a Sunday?	Would you rather be a chocolate chip cookie or a gummy bear?
Would you rather have chocolate or chips?	Would you rather drive a motorcycle or a fancy car?	Would you rather eat sushi or have a hot dog?	Would you rather cook breakfast or lunch?	Would you rather live in a cabin or a castle?
Would you rather be a cat or a dog?	Would you rather download music or movies?	Would you rather take the subway or the bus?	Would you rather have rich friends or funny friends?	Would you rather have a cup of tea or a cup of coffee?

Follow-Up Activity: Look up the lyrics of a classic song called "El Condor Pasa" (sometimes called "If I Could"), sung by a well-known 1960s folk-rock duo, Simon and Garfunkel.

Here are some lines from the song:

"I'd rather be a sparrow than a snail."

and

"I'd rather be a hammer than a nail."

and

"I would rather be a forest than a street."

Try to make up your own song with similar comparisons, then read it aloud to a friend. Have fun!

93. **Good for the Grammy**

Imagine you are a top singer and songwriter in the music industry. You've just been nominated for a prestigious Grammy Award and need to read an acceptance speech. Luckily your two good friends, Gavin and Jenn, are going to write two different drafts for you. It's up to you to pick which one to use!

Reach each of the following speeches to decide which one you want to use. Be sure to practice saying each one out loud. You'll have to read it to a large audience when you win. And you'll only have three minutes to say it!

1. **The Cool and Casual Speech**
   Hi, folks! Wow, wow, wow! This is a surprise. Cool man, real cool. This is a blast . . . wow, wow, wow. Just a few thanks. Bob, you are terrific, the best sound engineer in the world! Thanks, man. My backup group, I could not have done this without you. Thanks, Gladys, Gloria, and Jeff. Cool folks. Thanks to Jackie, my wonderful admin assistant, for the supply of coffee. You are great, Jackie, and please don't leave. We all need you! Thanks to the judges. You got it right at last! Ha, ha, ha. Good night, guys, and have a blast!

2. **The "I Don't Deserve This" Speech**
   No, no, this is unbelievable! What can I say? I do not deserve this. There is so much talent here tonight. I can't believe I get to take this trophy home! Thanks to my mom and dad, my brother, Josh, my sister, Carrie, and my backup group. You all deserve this award, not me! Thanks to my fans. You lift me up when all seems lost. The support I've gotten from you all has been amazing. I still can't believe this. Have a great evening and thanks again. Good night.

The target is to read your speech in less than 3 minutes. Try your speech three times, record your time each time you practice, and try to speed up a little each time.

	Time in Seconds	Time in Seconds	Time in Seconds
Speech 1			
Speech 2			
Final speech choice			

94. The School Magazine

You're the chief editor of the school magazine, and you want to encourage new writers, including students in younger grades, to contribute. You've received an interesting article from Hannah, who is in eighth grade and has not written an article before. Hannah is dyslexic and has difficulty with punctuation and verb tenses. She is very creative and very interested in being a writer.

Hannah's article is below. Your job is to correct it, then put it into a 75-word article for the magazine. Readers should be able to read it in five minutes. Start by correcting the grammar and sentences. Then, read it to yourself. Can you read it in five minutes? Try to take out some words so the article is only 75 words.

Suddenly I Froze

The trees rustled and made a loud swishing noise—swish, swish. I had to meet my friend for the basketball practice—at 6:30 am—yes that early but the school lights shone brightly so I used these to guide me along the narrow path to the school gate where Jannat was going to be waiting for me! I was wondering if I was imagining this but I heard all sorts of strange noises—squeaks and squawks—I stopped in my tracks whoosh—a sudden whooshing noise came out from the thick bramble bush. The Yap Yap sound was sudden and scary—then I froze as two timid looking cats hurled out from the bush fighting or playing (not sure which) by maybe playing as they seem to be having fun—at my expense!

_____

_____

_____

_____

_____

_____

_____

95. **Words of Inspiration**

Poetry has the power to move us, motivate us, and, most of all, inspire us. People were amazed by the moving and vivid words of National Youth Poet Laureate Amanda Gorman at President Joe Biden's inauguration on January 20, 2021. Reciting poetry (reading it out loud) can be good practice for fluent reading. Paying attention to the tempo, rhythm, and stress of certain words helps expression.

Find a video online of Amanda Gorman reciting her poem "The Hill We Climb." Notice how she speaks her words. When does she speed up or slow down? When does she pause or stop? When is her voice louder or softer? Are there certain words that stand out? These are all things that add to expression in reading.

Now, find a piece of poetry that inspires you and practice reading it. If you don't have any poetry books, go to PoetryFoundation.org, a great online resource to read and learn about poems.

96. Express Yourself

Expression is important for meaning as well as fluency. Before you read a passage, check for unknown or difficult words, and be aware of the key points as you read.

For this activity, imagine you are a soccer commentator, and you are commentating on an international game between the US and Canada.

Preparing to read with expression:

- Go through the passage below and write down all of the words you find difficult, such as the names of some players.
- Decode these words and practice saying them until you can do it automatically.
- Read the passage silently. Take your time. Do this a few times.
- Read the passage aloud; this is a practice read.
- Now, for the real thing! Read with expression and record your commentary.
- Replay it and think about how you might improve.
- Underline all the important words that you want to emphasize.
- For the final commentary, find an audience to read it to or record it again!

You are picking up this commentary midway through the second half of the tense international soccer game between Canada and the US. Sinclair, the Canadian team leader, accepts another great pass from Tancredi in the 67th minute. She cleverly slips the ball past Solo inside the right-hand post. But the US team is making a strong comeback. Rapinoe races up the field and blasts the ball high into the net via the post. It is a spectacular goal, and now the teams are tied at 2 to 2.

Now, here we are with only 15 minutes of the game left, and Canada is on the attack again. It is a corner quickly taken by Schmidt! Sinclair heads the ball cleanly into the top corner of the goal. It is 3 to 2 Canada, but the game is far from over.

The US makes a quick counterattack. The Canadian defender, Nault, handles the ball inside the area. It is a penalty. The handling offense seemed to be unintentional, but the penalty stands. Wambach makes no mistake and hammers the ball into the net. Now, at the end of the 90 minutes with the score 3 to 3, we are ready for extra time.

Here we are now in extra time, and the US team is pushing hard. The Canadian side looks exhausted, but they're fighting hard. We are now in the final minutes of extra time. O'Reilly for the US is charging up the wing and places a great cross onto the head of the leaping Morgan, who slides a header just inside the crossbar for a sensational late winner for the US, 4 to 3. What a game! The United States deserved to win this tough game, but experts would say so did Canada.

97. Breathe and Pause

You might want to get reading tasks over with as soon as possible, especially if you're reading aloud, but reading aloud is good practice for fluency. When you are reading aloud, remember to do these things:

- Pause for breath when the natural pauses occur in a sentence. Watch and listen carefully to news broadcasters and pay attention to when they pause in a sentence.
- Read all the words without hesitation.
- Emphasize some words and skip over others quickly.

For this activity, you'll be reading a familiar passage called "The African Leopard." (Remember Exercise 88 on page 96?) Here's what you'll do.

- Practice reading the passage to yourself.
- After you've practiced a few times and are sure you can read all the words, you are almost ready to read aloud.
- First, make sure you know the meaning of the words. Make a note of all the new words and find out what they mean.
- Now, you are ready to read aloud. Practice reading the passage aloud at least three times.
- Record yourself using your phone or computer. Remember to breathe and pause!
- Listen to the recording and think about how you might improve.

  - Did you read too fast or too slow?
  - Did you hesitate over any words?
  - Did you break for breath at the end of each sentence?
  - Did you differ the tone of your voice at any point? For example, did you speak louder or quieter?
  - Did you finish by your target time?

- Praise yourself for doing this activity! Remember to breathe and pause while reading aloud or even when you are reading to yourself.

The African Leopard

The African leopard can show a great deal of variation in coat color. This depends on where it is located. This is called the habitat. The color of the African leopard's coat varies from a pale yellow to a deep gold. There are also black leopards. Male leopards are usually larger than females. Some mountain leopards are smaller and less heavy than other leopards, but all leopards usually hunt at night.

98. Matching Phrases

Sometimes you are asked to fill in the blank or finish the sentence, so it's important to notice the relationships between words. Here is a quick review of the meaning of some joining words:

- Because: the reason for something
- But: used to show contrast or difference
- And: joining additional information
- So: shows the reason between two things
- For: a reason for something
- While: action happening at the same time
- Yet: similar to but, used to show slight difference
- After: showing time, occurring after something

For this activity, read the phrase in the first column and then pick the most appropriate middle word to connect the phrase to a different phrase in the last column. Once you have connected the two, read your complete sentence quickly and accurately.

The teacher told the class to sit	because	eventually it printed out the document.
The pizza was hot	and	his wife watched the news.
The senate refused to discuss the bill	for	the last bell rang at the end of the day.
	yet	I like milk chocolate as well.
The weather was cooperating	but	her mother put her to bed very early.
The doctor lost his tongue depressor	so	his friend was over an hour and a half late.
	but	they needed to take attendance.
The young child was very tired	while	extremely spicy.
The printer was stuck	after	it was in the House of Representatives for the last two years.
The man read the newspaper	and	
The student went to the café	because	it still felt like it might rain.
I love dark chocolate	but	was able to examine the patient's tonsils without it.
The student got very upset	so	
The young girl disliked reading	and	I still don't completely trust her.
The young married couple decided to move to another country	yet	I caught the 212 bus and was home earlier.
	because	they had to get new passports and work visas.
The movie ending was so good	so	
She is very nice and personable		the good guys won in the end.
Tim decided not to wait		she loved to create and write short stories.
The 211 bus didn't show up		he received a bad grade on his math test.

99. In Your Own Words

Have you ever read a sentence or a passage and then thought, "What does that mean?" Paraphrasing (or putting text into your own words) can help you summarize and understand what was written.

Practice reading the following sentences, then summarize them in your own words.

Example:

The fast, flowing river proved dangerous and treacherous for the kayaking group, so they were delegated to groups according to skill.

<u>The kayaks were put into separate groups because the water was dangerous.</u>

The temperature reached minus zero, and the biting wind blew right through the extra woolly layers that the young child wore.

_____

_____

The significant increase of greenhouse gases in Earth's atmosphere has been directly linked to global warming, and weather patterns are directly affected by this.

_____

_____

The current trend of young adults living at home until they reach their mid-30s has dramatically increased over the past two decades. This troubling trend has dire results on families and social networks.

_____

_____

One of the most significant economic trends in North America has been the sharp increase in the number of women returning to work, but they are suffering the ill effects of wage disparity.

_____

_____

The dramatic increase of vaping among teenagers has led experts to rethink legislation and current policies in each and every state in the country.

_____

_____

Reading-Comprehension Activities

100. Understanding Reading Comprehension

Reading comprehension is extremely important! What is the point in reading something if you do not understand it? Reading comprehension is how you interact with the text, how you interpret the text, and what the text means to you. A text can have different meanings to different people. What *you* think about the text is important, and you need to hold on to that. Of course, some texts may not be open to a wider interpretation and may have right or wrong answers. This section includes examples of both types of texts and introduces a variety of reading comprehension techniques.

Sometimes, understanding text is related to asking the right questions. This means that while you are reading, you need to be thinking about the meaning, too. In other words, you need to engage with the text. Ask yourself questions while you are reading and reflect on the text.

Why, What, Where, How

While you are reading, or at least immediately after you read, you need to ask yourself some questions. This activity focuses on "why," "what," "where," and "how" questions. These questions may not relate to every piece of text you read, but they can be very useful for lots of different types of texts. Read the following passage and answer the questions.

The Camino

Lucas stared at Noah in disbelief. "We have to walk the whole 100 kilometers?"

"Yes," Noah smirked. "But we have 10 days to do it."

Lucas and Noah were about to walk the last 100 kilometers of the famous Camino de Santiago. They were both excited. They had just graduated from high school and were ready for the next stage in their education. They thought that this was the time for a challenge like the famous Camino walk in Spain.

Several days before, Lucas and Noah flew from New York to Barcelona and then took a bus to Sarria where they met a group to begin the 10-day adventure! They intend to walk the section of the route called the Camino Frances. It stretches from Sarria to Santiago through the region of Galicia in northern Spain. In the upcoming days, Noah and Lucas will follow country roads and woodland paths until they reach the city of Amenal, near the end of the 10 days. After a night's rest, they will finally head for Santiago, the most exciting and final part of the walk. After all that walking, they will both receive a certificate and perhaps a few blisters, too! But right now, Lucas isn't so sure this is a great idea.

➡️

"Don't forget, Lucas, this is a pilgrimage, so it is not just walking. It will give us an opportunity to reflect on what we are doing and maybe even how we want to spend the next few years at college," Noah reminded his friend. He continued, "There is one phrase we will need to know, Lucas, and that is 'Buen camino!' It is the meet-and-greet phrase that pilgrims and locals use." Noah laughed.

"Okay, it will be fun," remarked Lucas.

The two friends headed off for a great adventure!

Use this passage to answer the following questions. It is a good idea to reread the passage a few times before answering the questions.

1. **Why** are they doing this?

   _____

   _____

2. **What** are they doing?

   _____

   _____

3. **Where** are they?

   _____

   _____

4. **How** are they going to do this?

   _____

   _____

101. **Dig This!**

Maya and Naomi left the movie theater and blinked rapidly. They were delighted. Naomi had said that the movie would be right up their alley, and it was. They both loved archaeology and had just watched a captivating movie called *The Dig*, which was filmed in England. They had never been to England, but they were fascinated by ancient history and the discoveries of cultures from long ago. They learned so much from the movie!

The Anglo-Saxons, the Vikings, and the Normans all invaded and lived in England, and the documentary explored their history. There were amazing finds in Scotland, too. In 2019, a large Norse hall, probably from the 10th to 12th centuries CE, was discovered at a farmstead on an island near Orkney in northwest Scotland. It is thought that the hall was used by a high-status leader. Many of the relics, like jewelry, were carefully transferred to national museums where they could be skillfully restored and displayed behind glass.

The Vikings in particular were skilled sailors and fearsome explorers. There are many relics of Viking brooches, ornaments, and long ships in museums across Europe. It is believed the Viking explorer Leif Erikson from Iceland was the first European to set foot in North America, 400 years before Christopher Columbus. Historical accounts, however, differ on exactly where he landed in North America as records at that time were usually passed down through generations by word of mouth. These oral records are often referred to as sagas and were written on scrolls centuries later. In the United States, October 9 is Leif Erikson Day in honor of the great explorer.

Stories like these really excited Maya and Naomi, who spend a lot of time visiting the many museums in the US. Some day they hope to visit the Viking World Museum in Iceland.

Questions

Before you begin answering the questions, make a list of the difficult words in the passage, then look up the meaning of each one. Some words you might want to look up are "fearsome," "archeology," "captivating," "status," "restored," "relics," "brooches," "sagas," and "scrolls."

1. What does the expression "right up their alley" mean? Why do you think Naomi said that?

_____

_____

2. Which groups of people invaded and lived in England?

_____

_____

➡

3. What is a relic? Can you give an example of a relic from the passage?

_____

_____

4. Why were the people of Orkney excited about the amazing find?

_____

_____

5. What is a saga?

_____

_____

6. What does "by word of mouth" mean?

_____

_____

7. Why do historical accounts differ on the arrival of Leif Erikson in America?

_____

_____

Follow-Up Activity: Google the Viking World Museum in Iceland. Check out the museum's website (VikingWorld.is) and make a list of some of the Viking relics that are on display there.

102. **Make It Short**

Summarizing is closely connected to reading comprehension. To summarize a passage, identify its key points. If you can summarize a text, you likely have a good understanding of it.

A Day to Remember

Everyone in 10th grade was excited about the soccer game on Saturday. It was the final game of the season! The match was between the Upstarts and the neighboring school's team, the Cedars. There had always been rivalry between the two teams, but there was rivalry within the Upstarts, too. They had some great players. Paul O'Grady was the top scorer, scoring 30 goals so far this season, and Jacob Smith was the second top scorer with 28 goals. So, there was a bit of a rivalry between Paul and Jacob.

The whole stadium buzzed with excitement! The cheerleaders energized the crowd, the local school band played some tunes, and before long, the game had started. It seemed like everyone in the stadium was counting on Paul and Jacob for a win. Fifteen minutes into the game, Paul led a breakaway and bulleted the ball high toward the goal. Jacob knew what was going to happen, so he sprinted to the inside edge of the penalty area. He met Paul's pass perfectly and was setting up for a shot when his legs were whipped out from under him by the Cedars's ruthless center back. It was a penalty, and the Cedars player received a warning yellow card for his reckless foul. The Cedars were determined to win even if they had to play unfairly. Paul and Jacob exchanged looks and knew what they would have to do. They would need to set aside their rivalry to win this game. It didn't matter who scored more goals. They needed to work together.

During the rest of the game, Paul and Jacob worked together to continue to score against the Cedars. The boys and the other Upstart players bravely held on until the final whistle. For the first time ever, the Upstarts had won the finals! Paul and Jacob tied for goals scored that season. What a day to remember!

For this activity, write a summary for your school paper. You are excited to let everyone know how exciting the game was. This passage contains over 300 words, but you need to summarize it in 50 words.

_____

_____

_____

_____

103. **The Ship of Dreams**

This passage is about the *Titanic* exhibition. Summarize the exhibition to your class.

The very name *Titanic* gives the impression of magnificence. The *Titanic* was magnificent! Work on the *Titanic* began in a shipyard in Belfast, Ireland, in 1909. It was a massive undertaking and was to be the greatest and most unsinkable ship ever to take to the waters. More than 100,000 people attended the launch in May 1911. To get an idea of how large the crowd was, consider that the crowd during the 2019 Super Bowl between the Los Angeles Rams and the New England Patriots at the Mercedes-Benz Stadium in Atlanta, Georgia, was approximately 70,000 people. Imagine the cheering from the 100,000-person crowd when the *Titanic* was launched.

The *Titanic* was described as unsinkable because it had a double bottom with 15 watertight compartments equipped with electric watertight doors that were operated manually or by a switch on the bridge. Years later, marine experts suggested that the watertight compartments contained a critical flaw. The walls separating the compartments were only a few feet above the waterline, and if the ship tilted, water could pour from one compartment to another, which is exactly what happened.

The other flaw was what we might call complacency. If a football team is winning easily over their opponents, the team may ease off a bit. They might become careless. This is what happened with the *Titanic*. They did not have nearly enough lifeboats for all the passengers on the ship.

On the fateful night of its maiden voyage from Southampton, England to New York, the *Titanic* struck an iceberg off the coast of Newfoundland and sank in a mere 2 hours and 40 minutes. It is believed that 1,500 people died in the freezing water. Miraculously, 706 people survived. The *Titanic* included people from all walks of life, from the wealthiest, who paid a small fortune to travel on the *Titanic*, to the less well-off, who paid as little as $15 (about $170 in today's money).

Stories of survival and harrowing tales of doom were passed on from that tragic night. The story of the *Titanic* is displayed in many museums and exhibitions around the country, and in the Oscar-winning movie *Titanic*.

Use the text to answer the following questions:

1. Why do you think the *Titanic* was called the "Ship of Dreams"?

_____

_____

2. Describe two flaws that contributed to the sinking of the *Titanic*.

_____

_____

3. What does the word "complacency" mean? Give two examples of complacency you may have experienced or know about.

_____

_____

4. What does the expression "harrowing tales of doom" mean?

_____

_____

5. Why do you think the *Titanic* is of great interest today?

_____

_____

6. What message do you think the story of the *Titanic* can give us in today's society?

_____

_____

104. What Reading Comprehension Is All About

Reading comprehension is a bit like detective work. You have to find out what the text means. Just like a detective looks for clues at a crime scene, you look for clues in a passage. You have to interpret the passage just as a detective has to interpret a crime scene. Read the passage below and answer the questions that follow.

Kate and Jake were eager hikers. They had already visited Yosemite National Park and considered it their special place. They often reminisced about the two weeks they spent there. Yosemite Falls was breathtaking, and they hiked the full seven miles to the top of the falls. Jake recalled how his heart was pounding as they summited the 2,700-foot climb. He was carrying the backpack! They were glad that they hiked during spring break because summer is a busy time at Yosemite, and during the winter, the trails can be treacherous. They were not beginners and always opted for the intermediate routes. There were notices all over the trail telling hikers what they could and could not do. One of the important notices said "No Campfires." At another place on the trail, there was a sign that said "No Dogs Allowed Beyond This Point." The views were phenomenal, and Kate clicked away merrily with her new camera and zoom lenses.

It was a fantastic trip for the duo, and they were closer friends now than ever before. They were about to set off to different colleges. Jake would be in New York, and Kate would be in California. It would be a sad parting, but they had happy memories. Of course, they'd always be able to meet up for another trip to their special place!

Questions

1. What evidence is there from the passage that Kate and Jake liked Yosemite Falls?

_____

2. Why was Jake's heart pounding? Give two reasons.

_____

3. Why did they choose to do the hike during their spring break?

_____

4. What does it mean when the passage says the trail up the falls was an intermediate route? What criteria do your think the park rangers would have for labeling a hike intermediate?

_____

5. Why does the passage refer to Kate and Jacob as a duo?

_____

6. Explain why the term "sad parting" was used in the passage.

_____

7. Where is Yosemite Falls?

_____

8. What two notices to hikers were mentioned in the passage?

_____

9. Can you figure out why these notices were important?

_____

10. Why do you think summer is a busy time at Yosemite National Park?

_____

105. **Read Between the Lines**

Some authors do not need to tell you everything that is happening because they have mentioned it earlier in the story or perhaps they assume you will know by the sense of the sentence. When this happens, you'll need to read between the lines or use context and background (previous) knowledge to help you understand the passage.

Practice reading between the lines with the following sentences. Then use the chart that follows to show the evidence that helped you make an inference.

1. Eight school backpacks were piled outside the back door of the house. When his mother arrived, she was fuming.

2. The car pulled up to the gate, and the driver produced his official ID.

3. The office worker held the bag of fast food carefully on his lap during the bus ride.

4. The baby cried when his mother left the room, but he also cried when she returned later that day!

5. The band played the intro to the song six times before the vocalist scurried on stage.

Evidence from the Text	Inferences
school backpacks piled at door	The mother was not expecting other children to be invited home. Or she was annoyed at the backpacks not being in a tidy row or hung up.

106. **Making Predictions**

One way to know whether you understand a passage is if you can predict what might happen next.

Complete the three sentences below by trying to make appropriate predictions. For the first three questions, underline the one from the list that seems the most likely. Then, complete the rest of the unfinished sentences. Make your own prediction of what might happen next.

1. The car driver was irate _____.

    a. when he was feeling happy

    b. when the pedestrian rushed from the sidewalk

    c. when the newspapers were on sale

    d. when Aunt Jessie was home at last

2. The school day was over, and _____.

    a. we kept reading our books

    b. the table toppled

    c. we ran to the school bus

    d. his new sweater looked great

3. He crept around the corner, clinging to the wall, and spotted bright shadows from the eerie darkness, then _____.

    a. suddenly he stopped and took his wallet out

    b. he froze at the sudden screeching noise

    c. a firework lit up the sky

    d. it was election night

Now write your own prediction about what happened next:

1. He studied every night for the history exam and discussed some practice questions with his friends, so it was no surprise _____.

➡

2. The soccer player skillfully weaved past the opponents, but unfortunately

_____.

3. The vocalist looked at his drummer with a puzzled expression

_____.

4. Katherine was bored and decided to make some cookies. After mixing the dough carefully, she placed the cookies on the baking tray and into the hot oven. Then her friend rang the doorbell. Katherine excitedly jumped in the air and ran to the door

_____.

5. The two boys had been fishing all day and had started to feel

_____.

6. The new boutique on Main Street was _____.

7. Amos was feeling nervous because today _____.

107. **Debatable Debates**

No matter the topic, there is usually more than one way of looking at it. Most topics or ideas are open to debate. This exercise includes two arguments about technology, specifically the question, "Is technology making us smarter?" You might already have an opinion about this question, but consider both sides of the argument. Read the two arguments carefully and then answer the questions.

Is technology making us smarter?

For:

Yes, technology is making us smarter. Technology allows us to have a world of knowledge at our fingertips. We can use it to acquire knowledge and information easily and learn new skills. We can even diagnose some of our illnesses or medical issues using technology. Technology has brought history alive, geography to our doorstep, and science into our lives. We know more about the past now and can learn more about other countries, nations, and customs. Everyone in society has benefited from technology. Software can guard our homes, protect our children, and help us design new buildings and homes. Thank you, technology.

Against:

Technology has made us less intelligent. We let technology do our thinking and our research and often rely on it to solve our problems. We spend most of our free time on our computers. In some cases, they're our best friends. You might argue that technology can even cause social isolation and social inadequacies.

The expression, "The grass is always greener on the other side" is one that can apply to social media, a product of technology. When they use social media, people compare themselves to others, which contributes to feelings of dissatisfaction. Technology can influence people without them even knowing it. It can track our movements, our likes and dislikes, and even where we are at any moment in time! Technology takes away our freedom and privacy.

Questions

1. Write one argument for the use of technology and one against it.

_____

2. What is meant by "new skills," and how can technology help?

_____

➡️

3. Do you agree that everyone in society has benefited from technology? Give some examples to support your answer.

_____

4. Can you think of some other arguments for and against technology? Try to give two examples of each.

_____

5. If this were a debate, who do you think would win and why?

_____

Tips and Tools

There are many different strategies to improve memory and develop memorization skills. One of these might work for you. You can think of memorization techniques like tactics in a football game—strategies to help you win.

- **Make time for repetition.** Give yourself opportunities for repetition to reinforce what you are learning. The goal in reviewing what you've learned isn't to just memorize but to understand it. Use the new learning in notes or discussions, or you can jot down some key points from it.

- **Organize the information.** Organization is important for memory. The key to organizing information is to rearrange the information so you can more easily understand it. One way to do this is to use headings and subheadings in your notes. Creating your own visual representation of an idea can also reinforce a concept. Both strategies will help you personalize your learning.

- **Keep good notes.** Label notes with the dates you wrote them. This helps you organize and recall the information.

- **Make sure you understand the information.** Ask yourself questions about the information until you are sure you know why you studied it. This will help with comprehension.

- **Be confident.** There is no such thing as a bad memory, just ineffective strategies or no strategies. With the right strategies, you can remember what you need and want to remember.

Reading and Writing Skills

108. **In Your Own Words**

Many students with dyslexia have an excellent imagination and a rich oral vocabulary. Putting those ideas into writing, though, can be challenging. Fortunately, there are many strategies available to help develop reading and writing skills.

When writing an essay, you often have to research information and use quotes or references. Paraphrasing (putting what someone else has said into your own words) is an excellent skill to learn for high school writers.

Tips for paraphrasing:

- Circle important words that help demonstrate the main idea or crucial facts connected to the main idea.
- Circle words that you feel are important and think of words you know that are similar to them.
- Use "wh" questions to frame your rewrite. For example: Who is this about? When did it happen? Why did it happen or why is this important? Where did it take place?

Practice paraphrasing the quotes in the chart. If it is difficult, try using some of the tips. Use a thesaurus or a dictionary if you need to in order to understand some of the quotes.

Quotes	Paraphrase
"The spread of the virus can be directly linked to the amount of international travel, which causes the new variants of the virus to be transmitted to the public at large."	
"The single most deadly strain to date has been linked to overseas variants. Public health measures have not been mandated or reinforced in some countries."	
"The WHO (World Health Organization) argues that the lack of transparency and reporting along with social and economic inequities will have a severe impact on who receives vaccines first and the rate at which a country's population can develop herd immunity."	

109. The Rich and Famous

Here is the chance of a lifetime! You get to read about three famous people and then interview one of them. Read the following bios of some famous people and then create five questions that you would want to ask them. Write your questions on the lines provided.

Born September 26, 1981, Serena Williams is one of America's most beloved and well-known tennis players. She began her career early by learning tennis from her father and turned professional in 1995. Since then, she has gone on to win 23 Grand Slam titles and Olympic medals for her tennis playing. She gave birth to her daughter and was married in 2017. She still continues to play tennis today. Her autobiography *On the Line* was published in 2009.

Born Aubrey Drake Graham in Toronto, Canada, on October 24, 1986, Drake has become a major influencer in the music industry. He first gained popularity in the teen drama series *Degrassi: The Next Generation* (2001–2007). Drake wanted to pursue a career in the music industry and released his first studio album *Thank Me Later* in 2010, which topped the US Billboard 200 chart. Drake cofounded OVO Sound in 2012. He has won four Grammy Awards, five American Music Awards, and six Juno Awards.

Born in 1994 in Stratford, Ontario, Justin Bieber is a Canadian singer and songwriter. Bieber was discovered on YouTube when his mom posted clips to the site. In 2009, his album *My World* went platinum. After a period out of the spotlight, he made a comeback in 2015 and went on to break records for the most consecutive weeks at number 1 in the top 100. In 2020, he broke another record as for the seventh time, as one of his albums reached the top spot on the Billboard 200 chart.

My interview choice is _____.

List of Five Questions:

1. _____

2. _____

3. _____

4. _____

5. _____

110. **Checking with Pros and Cons**

This activity will help you think critically and make judgments based on your views or on the evidence. This is good for comprehension, critical thinking, analyzing, and writing.

The statements below can be considered controversial. That means there is usually more than one opinion about the situation.

When you consider different points of view, you might think in terms of pros and cons. The expression "pros and cons" is from Latin—"pro" (for) and "contra" (against)—and has been used in this way since the 16th century.

Read the following statements and write a pro and con for each one.

1. We drive on the right side of the road, but some other countries drive on the left side. We should make motorists in every country drive on the right.

Pros _____

Cons _____

2. In 2019, a change was made to the National Hockey League rulebook. It said, "A player who loses his helmet will have to go to the bench or put the helmet back on properly before playing." Is this fair?

Pros _____

Cons _____

3. Homework should be abolished!

Pros _____

Cons _____

4. Public transit should be free for everyone, everywhere.

Pros _____

Cons _____

111. **Magazine Article**

The challenge of writing a magazine article is that the important information needs to be summarized and the interesting points need to be included, but often editors only allow a certain number of words. Being able to summarize in an effective and succinct (short) way is an important skill. Paraphrasing (using your own words as much as possible) is important as well.

Write a 60-word article for *Pets Monthly Magazine* using the following information about a puppy. Include the title of your magazine article and make the article interesting.

My name: Hamish

My nickname: Famous Hamish, Love Bug

My breed: Border collie

My age: 7.5 months

My favorite things to do: Snuggle with my mom, sit in puddles, try to steal slippers when no one is looking, harass my dad, and play, play, play! I'm in charge of the "Neighborhood Watch" because I love to look out the window and see what everyone is doing.

My favorite food: Puppy kibbles, turkey bites, cookies

My favorite toy: Because I'm part Scottish, I love sheep. My favorite "stuffies" are called Baba Sheep and McCloud. I love all "stuffies" and socks and bones, of course. I can chew for hours!

What I hate the most: When I'm home alone! I cry like a baby! I also hate vacuum cleaners, squirting sounds from bottles, and, of course, baths. I don't need a bath. I smell good the way I am!

Do I like car rides? Of course, I do. I love to drive! Only joking. Ha ha.

Do I snore? I snuffle; I don't snore.

Hamish the Wonder Puppy

_____

_____

_____

112. **Photo-Telling**

There is an expression that people often use: "A picture is worth a thousand words." Even just a glimpse at an image can quickly convey bits of information to you.

Write a short story about each of the two images in this activity. Be creative and use your imagination.

Here are some questions to think about:

- What is happening?
- What are the facial expressions showing about the person's feelings?
- Where is it happening?
- What are the clues about the event?
- How do you think it might end?

_____

_____

_____

_____

_____

_____

_____

113. **Sell It!**

Your advertisement agency has been chosen to write an advertisement for a new product. Based on the information provided by the agency, write a TV commercial for the product. Your advertisement should be at least 50 words long.

Words that describe the product:

- Breathable
- Water-resistant
- Mesh tops
- Memory foam liners with spring bottoms
- Lightweight
- Shock-absorbing
- Ideal for short- or long-distance running
- Long-wearing
- Odor-repelling

_____

_____

_____

_____

_____

_____

114. **Dear Reader**

Good advice never goes out of style. "Dear Abby" is a famous newspaper column that gives readers wise advice for their everyday problems.

For this activity, read the following letter and give a response for your "Dear Reader" column series. Make sure to provide thoughtful advice to your loyal readers!

My family is usually very supportive of me, but lately we have been fighting over what I should study at college. I would like to study engineering because I am very good at math and science, but my mom and dad would prefer I study law and become a lawyer. We are at odds over this, and it has sometimes caused some big fights between me and my parents. I feel like they are trying to control me, and the idea of becoming a lawyer is unbearable. What should I do?

Signed,

Destined to Be an Engineer

Your response:

_____

_____

_____

_____

115. **Just the Gist!**

Getting the gist of something means that you can get the big idea of what is going on, even if there is a lot of information coming your way. Being able to quickly identify topics and the main idea in a paragraph is a good skill to have.

For this activity, you will practice picking out important pieces of information, such as the main idea, and writing down words and evidence that support your thinking.

Looking at Global Warming

Global warming is a phenomenon of Earth's average air temperature increasing over the last two centuries. Scientists have speculated about the existence of global warming since the beginning of the industrial revolution. One of the biggest factors in global warming is CO_2 emissions, as a by-product of human activities. Scientists have long warned of the devastation that global warming can produce. They cite current extreme weather patterns and natural disasters as a result of climate change due to global warming.

Topic: _____

Main idea: _____

Words that support the main idea: _____

Facts/evidence/ideas from the passage that support the main idea: _____

_____

_____

_____

_____

_____

_____

116. **Did You Know?**

Fun facts are interesting to many people, especially those who love to be amazed by how many unique world records there are.

For this activity, visit the Guinness World Records website and read several amazing or weird facts. Then, write two or three amazing "Did You Know?" facts of your own!

To get you started, take a look at one of the most well-known success stories in the Black community: the journey of Madam C. J. Walker. Then write a short summary of the journey she made.

Did You Know?

The highest-earning movie worldwide is James Cameron's film *Avatar*. The movie *Avengers: Endgame* is the second highest, earning a whopping $2.5 billion as of July 2019.

Did You Know?

The most expensive *Star Wars* action figure ever sold was at an online action on July 11, 2019. The Boba Fett rocket-firing action figure sold for $185,850. The figurine, which was originally designed in 1979 to go along with the *Empire Strikes Back* release, was shelved due to safety concerns. That's a lot of money for a little piece of *Star Wars*!

Did You Know?

_____

_____

_____

Did You Know?

_____

_____

_____

Did You Know?

_____

_____

_____

117. **A Picture Is Worth a Thousand Words**

The old saying "A picture is worth a thousand words" (as previously discussed on page 130) is never more true than when you are trying to sell or promote something.

For this activity, write a travel brochure based on the images below. Make sure to research the area, then think of descriptive words to describe your location.

Here are some useful headings you can use:

- Places to Visit
- Language(s) Spoken
- Climate

Ireland

_____   _____   _____

_____   _____   _____

_____   _____   _____

_____   _____   _____

_____   _____   _____

_____   _____   _____

118. **Just the Right Word**

Many movies and plays are based on books. The key to adapting a book is to write a great script that catches the feeling or spirit of the characters and what they are experiencing.

Based on the following synopsis, create a one-page script. Remember to capture the feelings, the environment, and the details of the place, time, and characters.

Synopsis

Characters: Two best friends, both in high school, both 17 years old.

Scenario: One friend just found out she has failed her end-of-school science exam. Now she won't be able to get into the college she wants to go to. The other friend has been accepted into a well-known science program at a very prestigious school. They will have to go their separate ways.

Setting: An empty hallway by a locker.

Script

_____

_____

_____

_____

_____

_____

_____

_____

119. **A Head Start**

Sometimes it's hard to start off a piece of writing because you don't know how to start, but the more you practice, the easier it gets.

This activity helps with practicing sentence skills. Write a sentence using the prompt on every day of the month. By the end of the month, you should have a complete set of sentence starters or strategies you can use. You may not have a book or paper you are currently writing; that's okay. Just practice using these starters so that you feel more comfortable.

The author shows this by…	On the other hand,…	For example,…	Unlike the _____, this article shows…	The first reason is…	This article indicates that…	To prove this to the reader, the author uses…
On page ___ of the book, the author shows this by…	In conclusion, the book shows…	The following quote demonstrates that…	In conclusion…	To start with, the author…	One of the most important themes is…	Overall, it is easy to see that…
In this article, it shows that…	One of the main arguments presented in this article is…	This is true because…	There are several reasons why…	The final reason for this is…	There are several factors that indicate this…	In order to _____, it's first necessary to…
Last but not least…	The author has shown…	During this time…	This quote shows that…	During the…	In addition to _____, this also shows that…	This example clearly illustrates…

120. **Be the Teacher!**

You have just been tasked with being the teacher for the day and are in charge of making a quiz for your class. Read the following article, and based on this article, create a quiz. It should have five questions.

Dolphins

Dolphins are widely regarded today for their playfulness, intelligence, and fun-loving ways. A dolphin may be considered any mammal from the toothed whales that may belong to the Delphinidae (oceanic dolphins) or the Platanistidae or Iniidae family. There are nearly 40 species of dolphins, six of which are commonly called whales. This includes killer whales and pilot whales.

Most dolphins are small in length and have spindle-shaped bodies and a beak-like snout with simple needle-like teeth. The bottlenose dolphin is the most common dolphin known to humans. They are well-known because of their built-in smiles, but also for their amazing ability to communicate via a large range of sounds and ultrasonic pulses. Studies have shown that dolphins have the longest social memories of any nonhuman species. Several members were able to recognize unique whistles associated with other dolphins they had been separated from for over 20 years.

Dolphins may live in either salt water or fresh water. Their territory ranges from equatorial to subpolar salt water, and they can be found in many major river systems. Dolphins are social mammals, which means they live in schools of five to several thousand members. They are carnivores and live on smaller fish found within their natural environments. Based on the fossils found, dolphins first appeared 16 to 23 million years ago during the Miocene epoch. These fossils provide scientists with a way to trace the dolphin line and help us understand these amazing and fascinating creatures.

My Questions for the Quiz:

1. _____

2. _____

3. _____

4. _____

5. _____

Answer Key

Phonics and Phonemic Awareness

Exercise 1: Vowels vs. Consonants

Famous Person	Vowels in Their Name (A, E, I, O, U)	Consonants in Their Name
Will Smith	ii	wll smth
Tom Hanks	o a	tm hnks
Morgan Freeman	oa eea	mrgn frmn
Miley Cyrus	ie u	mly cyrs
Lady Gaga	a aa	ldy gg
Justin Bieber	ui iee	justn bbr
Mariah Carey	aia ae	mrh cry
Justin Timberlake	ui ieae	tmbrlk
Leonardo DiCaprio	eoao iaio	lnrd dcpr
Michael Jordan	iae oa	mchl jrdn
Paul McCartney	au ae	pl mcrtny
Dwayne Johnson	ae oo	dwyn jhnsn
Sandra Bullock	aa uo	sndr bllck
Kanye West	ae e	kny wst
Eddie Murphy	eie u	dd mrphy
Adam Sandler	aa ae	dm sndlr
Samuel L. Jackson	aue ao	sml l jcksn
Jennifer Aniston	eie aio	jnnfr nstn

Exercise 2: Make the Syllable
headphones: 2; bicycle: 3; football: 2; keyboard: 2; television: 4; guitar: 2; skateboard: 2; sneaker: 2

Exercise 3: Take a Break

come/back; de/fens/ive; tack/le; scrim/mage; safe/ty; out/side; line/back/er; mid/dle

Exercise 4: Blend the Positions

backfield
tackle
center
quarterback
football
receiver
scrimmage
running
offensive

Exercise 5: Rhyme Production

frog; nose; wait; team

Exercise 6: Match the Rhymes

Game/same; neat/meet; bark/shark; crumpet/trumpet; chick/quick; care/pair; grapple/apple; flick/sick; rug/mug; looter/computer; boot/suit; crew/brew; took/look; bun/fun; angle/bangle; goal/soul; rookie/cookie; more/score; has/jazz; so/low

Exercise 9: Common Vowel Patterns

Vowel Pattern	Clue	Word
AY	Have a good one!	day
AY	The month before June	May
EA	A treat is to ___	eat
AI	It falls from the sky	rain
EE	Arranging to see friends	meet
OA	Body wash	soap
OA	A sailor sails in a ___	boat

Exercise 10: Vowel Patterns

Short vowel	Long vowel
bat	bait
sad	seed
twin	twine
bit	bite
cub	cube

Exercise 11: Short Vowels

Long Vowel	Short Vowel
tube	tub
cane	can
mane	man
plane	plan
dime	dim

Exercise 12: Short and Long U

Short U	Long U
dud	dude
mut	mute
cut	cute
us	use
tub	tube

Short and Long I

Long I	Short I
pipe	pip
kite	kit
bite	bit
stripe	strip
mite	mitt

Exercise 13: Beat the Clock

clock	cuff	ant	shrug	vet	zoo	lean	us
pup	muck	weak	score	home	duck	gut	stump
truck	fume	him	wimp	pug	sum	plus	suit
Pete	cup	lead	vote	pen	June	zen	muck
cub	deal	sell	blast	bean	game	duck	track
peek	shrub	wet	main	luck	hut	feel	beg
tell	jean	hem	lose	hum	den	pun	yet
glue	open	fruit	gum	goal	shrimp	Jen	yes
jug	mute	nut	seal	fuss	lump	coal	rut

Exercise 14: Blend It Up

Blends (Make As Many As You Can)	Word Using This Blend
ST, STR, TR	stop, strip, trip
CL, CR	clap, crust
TR, FR	trip, frog
BL, BR	blunt, brunt
ST, STR	stunt, strut
FR, FL	frump, floss
GL, GR	gloss, grunt
STR, ST	strike, stuck
SP, PT	spit, crept
SP, SM, MP	spot, smug, bump
PR, FR	prop, fret

Exercise 16: Consonant Digraphs

fish: SH
chip: CH
chocolate: CH
shamrock: SH
telling time/when: WH

Exercise 17: Blends vs. Digraphs

Consonant Digraph Team	Consonant Blend Team
Meesh	Drummond
Seesh	Blast
Sketch	Frond
Flash	Whendle
Drodge	Vestrand
Dereck	
Smith	

Exercise 18: Sound Deletion
cupcake: cake
popcorn: corn
snowman: man
lipstick: stick

Exercise 19: Final Sound Detection
window: /o/
plant: /t/
perfume: /m/
net: /t/
hoop: /p/

Exercise 20: Take the Pop Quiz!

1. C

2. B

3. C

4. C

5. A

6. C

7. A

8. false

9. C

10. true

Syllables and Multiple-Syllable Words

Exercise 21: Count the Syllables
- he/li/cop/ter: 4
- foot/ball: 2
- gui/tar: 2
- chair: 1
- cell/phone: 2
- pen: 1

Exercise 22: Silly Syllables

Word	Number of Syllables	Syllable Parts
estaboric	4	es/ta/bor/ic
yogonda	3	yo/gon/da
barrasa	3	bar/ra/sa
wundolul	3	wun/do/lul
farinic	3	fa/ri/nic
sotepic	3	so/tep/ic
toreptic	3	to/rep/tic
pranafam	3	pra/na/fam
jogilic	3	jog/il/ic
anermas	3	an/er/mas
trepal	2	tre/pal
sastac	2	sas/tac
lulocal	3	lu/loc/al
preham	2	pre/ham

Exercise 23: The Six Types of Syllables
Examples:
- Closed Syllables: blast, bend, fetch
- Open Syllables: hi, open, tiger
- Consonant + LE Syllables: crumble, humble, pimple
- Vowel/Consonant/E Syllables: stove, bake, joke
- R-Controlled Syllable: star, torn, bird
- Vowel Team Syllables: fleet, bean, nail

Exercise 24: Closed Syllables

Word	Yes: Closed Syllable	No: Not a Closed Syllable
blast	✔	
hi		✔
snap	✔	
me		✔
met	✔	
truck	✔	
she		✔
flat	✔	
it	✔	
he		✔
shrimp	✔	

Exercise 25: Spot the Open Syllable

mu/sic	sped	**she**	blend
de/cide	**de**/pend	shrimp	**be**/gin
nest	glad	**si**/lo	best
be	drifting	invest	**me**
dust	**I**	draft	include
de/lay	maze	**o**/pen	help
rust	**ha**/lo	jump	**ti**/ger

Exercise 30: Syllable Division: Where to Divide Words

Word	Division	Syllable Type
metal	met/al	robin
hotel	ho/tel	pony
dentist	den/tist	rabbit
poet	po/et	lion
complex	com/plex	monster
contest	con/test	rabbit

Exercise 36: Multisyllabic Mastery

Name of Player	Team	Name of Player	Team
Jaylen Brown (1)	Cel/tics (2)	Anthony Da/vis (2)	Lak/ers (2)
Gordon Hay/ward (2)	Nets (1)	LeBron James (1)	Heat (1)
Marcus Smart (1)	Ca/va/liers (3)	Dwight How/ard (2)	Bucks (1)
Jayson Ta/tum (2)	Nug/gets (2)	Kyle Kuz/ma (2)	Pel/i/cans (3)
Kemba Wal/ker (2)	War/ri/ors (3)	JaVale Mc/Gee (2)	Thun/der (2)
Kevin Du/rant (2)	Rock/ets (2)	Jimmy But/ler (2)	Sev/en/ty Six/ers (5)
Kyrie Ir/ving (2)	Pac/ers (2)	Bam A/de/bay/o (4)	Suns (1)
Joe Har/ris (2)	Clip/pers (2)	Khris Mid/dle/ton (3)	Trail Blaz/ers (3)
Klay Thomp/son (2)	War/ri/ors (3)	Devon Boo/ker (2)	Wiz/ards (2)
Stephen Cur/ry (2)	War/ri/ors (3)	Damian Lil/lard (2)	Trail Blaz/ers (3)
James Har/den (2)	Nets (1)	Harrison Barnes (1)	Kings (1)
Russell West/brook (2)	Wiz/ards (2)	DeMar De/Ro/zen (3)	Spurs (1)
Malcolm Brog/don (2)	Pac/ers (2)	LaMarcus Ald/ridge (2)	Spurs (1)
Victor O/lad/i/po (4)	Heat (1)	Derrick White (1)	Spurs (1)
Myles Tur/ner (2)	Pac/ers (2)	Kyle Low/ry (2)	Rap/tors (2)

Exercise 37: Syllable Types
- Closed Syllables: Butler, Drummond, Brogdon
- Open Syllables: Davis, Tatum, Oladipo, Lopez
- Consonant + LE Syllables: Create your own
- Vowel/consonant/E Syllables: Love, White, James, Mike
- R-Controlled Syllables: Butler, Walker, Booker, Turner, Harris
- Vowel Team Syllables: Brown, Green, Joe, Plumlee, Beal

Exercise 38: Rules and Tips for Dividing Syllables

Syllables	Example	Example	Example
Between two consonants	tur/nip	kit/ten	muf/fin
Usually after first consonant	de/pend		
Between compound words	work/out	home/work	base/ball
Between vowels if they make separate sounds	di/et	fu/el	po/et
Before consonant + LE	ket/tle	ta/ble	pim/ple

Exercise 39: Take the Pop Quiz!!

1. vowel sound

2. 3

3. A vowel team syllable is when two vowels work as a team to make one syllable sound in a word.

4. A closed syllable is when the vowel is a short vowel protected or closed in by one or more consonants as in the word **blast**.

5. because you usually only hear the R sound and not the vowel

6. Examples
- VC/CV: rab/bit, ten/nis
- V/CV: po/ny, o/pen
- VC/V: rob/in, cab/in
- VC/CCV or VCC/CV: mon/ster, pump/kin
- CV/VC: li/on, fu/el

7. C

8. B

9. Example: trans/for/ma/tion (4)

10. Answers will vary

Prefixes, Suffixes, Base Words, and Root Words

Exercise 40: Word Sort

Word	Base Word	Prefix	Suffix
happiness	happy		NESS
displace	place	DIS	
sociable	social		ABLE
games	game		S
joyful	joy		FUL
cupful	cup		FUL
matted	mat		ED
lovely	love		LY
doing	do		ING
undo	do	UN	
covering	cover		ING
uncover	cover	UN	

Exercise 41: Back to Base Words

Word	Base Words	Words with a Prefix or Suffix
impossible		impossible (prefix)
do	do	
read	read	
restless		restless (suffix)
pack	pack	
deck	deck	

➡

Word	Base Words	Words with a Prefix or Suffix
friend	friend	
dismiss		dismiss (prefix)
replay		replay (prefix)
run	run	
berries		berries (suffix)
cart	cart	
trapped		trapped (suffix)

Exercise 42: Preparing for Prefixes

Possible words:

- depend
- mistake
- imperfect
- overdone
- detour
- into
- impossible
- miscue
- unjust
- decamp
- unhappy
- miscue
- preamble
- replay

Exercise 43: Prefixes Change the Meaning

Word	Meaning	With Prefix	Meaning
light	something bright	delight	a state of happiness
vent	air opening	prevent	to stop
come	gather round	become	to make
act	to do something	overact	exaggerated expression

Word	Meaning	With Prefix	Meaning
act	to pretend	react	to act again
equal	same	unequal	not the same
appear	see	reappear	to see again
appear	see	disappear	to not see again
side	around	beside	close to
sense	reasonable	nonsense	not reasonable
place	put down	misplace	put in wrong place
do	to carry out a task	undo	to change the task
visible	to see	invisible	to not see
fix	to make better	prefix	preparing to make better

Exercise 44: Suffixes: You Can Do It!

Word	With Suffix	Meaning
music (noun)	musical (adjective)	good at music
music	musician	someone who plays a musical instrument
jump	jumpy	nervous
skip	skipper	someone who skips; person in charge of a boat
hand	handful	a lot of
spot	spotless	very clean
home	homeless	nowhere to stay
mad	madly	how mad the person is
in	inward	on the inside
hope	hopeful	having a lot of hope
inform	informative	having a lot of information

Exercise 46: Circle for Success

streamed / (streaming)
inline / (online)
unreal-time / (real-time)
(download) / downsize
response / (responsibility)
(principal) / principality
(music) / musical
(outlets) / inlets
outcome / (income)
(presently) / present
(access) / accessible
(whenever) / however
(insatiable) / satiable
(obtain) / detain

Exercise 49: Final E Spelling Rule

Drop the E (trash): driving, baked, chasing, broken, shakable
Keep the E (safe): graceless, brides, hopeful

Exercise 50: Double or Nothing

Base word	Suffix	One Syllable	Short Vowel	One Final Consonant	Suffix Starts with a Vowel	Word
sit	ing	emoji	emoji	emoji	emoji	sitting
grab	ed	emoji	emoji	emoji	emoji	grabbed
grow	ing	emoji	no emoji	emoji	emoji	growing
kick	ing	emoji	emoji	no emoji	emoji	kicking
stream	ing	emoji	no emoji	emoji	emoji	streaming
seat	ed	emoji	no emoji	emoji	emoji	seated
eat	ing	emoji	no emoji	emoji	emoji	eating

Exercise 51: Spelling: Final Y Rule and Word Search

joyful
pitiful
toying
denied
replied
easier
tiniest
prettiest
happiness
conveyed

Exercise 52: Know Your Roots

Greek: phonograph, chemistry, psychology, gym, phonology
Latin: bankrupt, connection, abruptly, ejected, collected, eruption, interruption, prescription, dictate

Exercise 53: Suffixes: More Than Just an Ending

1. graceful / adjective

2. excited / adjective

3. informative / adjective

4. waited / verb

5. changed / verb

6. icing / noun

7. subtraction / noun

8. articles / noun

9. biggest / adjective

10. mindless / adjective

Exercise 54: Detective Work 101

re: to do again
pre: before
sub: below or under
un: not or opposite
mid: middle of
ex: out from or away from
mis: wrong or bad
pro: forward
trans: across or through
bi: two

Exercise 55: Rainbow Corners

Possible words: unlocked, misreading, subtracting, conscripting, microphone, subtracting, overheated, biography

Exercise 56: Kicking Rules!

1.1.1. Doubling Rule: dotting, spotting, butted, swimming, letting, batting, dubbed, funny, wetting, biggest
Final E Rule: striving, replacing, braver, craved, removing, reserving, skating, stored, making, piping, having, likable, adorable
Final Y Rule: denied, replied, fried, cried, complied, craziest, copied

Exercise 58: Roll and Build
Examples:

1. instruct, pretext, happiness, biography, exhale, hugs

2. driver, biggest, reroll, transport, inform, instruct

3. jumped, jumping, retracted, introspecting, prohibit, bicycle

4. unhelpful, careless, joyful, messy, session, departing

5. react, overwhelm, undercharge, carefree, communism, extremist

6. intersect, triangle, inspect, mistake, midway, transparent

Exercise 59: Take the Pop Quiz!

1. a unit of meaning at the end of a word

2. a unit of meaning that comes at the beginning of a word

3. a unit of meaning that comes in the middle of word and contains the meaning of the word

4. C

5. A

6. A

7. A

8. C

9. B

10. A

Word Recognition

Exercise 60: Word Recognition and Sight Words

1. who

2. from

3. where

4. there

5. people

6. through

7. enough

8. said

9. often

10. busy

11. which

12. beautiful

13. pretty

14. island

Exercise 62: Nonsense or Not
table
laugh
warm
bird
corn
bring
draw
done
eye

Exercise 64: Word Within a Word
Possible smaller words:
combination: bin, comb, nation, tan, not
embarrassment: sent, bar, embarrass, ten, rant, bent, ember
hypothyroidism: thyroid, pot, rod, thy, posh, hot
geographical: graph, gap, peg, lip, rag
spectator: rot, sport, cat, taco, cop, set

Exercise 65: Unpacking Words
mis/place/ed
un/lock/ed
im/port/ant
re/pack/ing
re/send/ing
in/sert/ing
con/tain/ment
ex/clud/ing
un/focus/ed
un/finish/ed

Exercise 66: Sight Word Sort
Sight words: have, said, friend, Wednesday, they, what, were, give, people, because, once, who
Non-sight words: made, glad, drinking, at, him, we, helping, nest, eating, she, spoon, her

Exercise 73: Know Your Lane
Beginning: MIS, RE, PRE, DE, IN, UN
Middle: stand, quick, print, part, kick, spell, drink, trust, STRUCT, TRACT, like, bless, hope, care, play
End: ENT, TION, ION, MENT, ING, ED, LY, FUL, LESS, ER, EST, ANT, IC, S, NESS, ES

Exercise 74: Positional Spellings

he__ (**DGE**, J) ki__ (**CK**, C) sta__(**CK**, C) loun__(**GE**, J) star__(CK, **K**) coa__(**CH**, TCH)
__ump (**J**, DGE) not_(**TCH**, CH) bla__(**CK**, C) do__(**DGE**, J) _ilt (**K**, C) _ing (**K**, C)
fu__(**DGE**, GE) sna__(**CK**, K) du___(**TCH**, CH) spi__e (**CK**, K) de__(K, **CK**) __amp(K, **C**)
bi__e (**K**, CK) smu__ (**DGE**, J) bar__(**GE**, DGE) __em (**G**, J) clo__(**CK**, K) clu___(CH, **TCH**)

Exercise 75: Find the Sight Word

1. again

2. tongue

3. February

4. said

5. two

6. often

7. your

8. friend / gone

9. what / business

10. often / February

11. enough

12. because

13. toward

14. something / two

15. to / what

Exercise 77: Blend a Family
Examples:
ALL: small, call, tall, hall
ING: thing, bling, bring, fling
ONG: thong, tong, wrong
UNG: hung, sprung
ANG: hang, sprang, tang, sprang
INK: shrink, think, blink, brink
UNK: clunk, drunk, hunk
ANK: thank, shrank, clank, drank
ONK: clonk, honk, wonk

Exercise 78: Reading the Signs
Clockwise, from top left:

1. only

2. closed

3. limit

4. away

5. the

6. weight

7. wrong

Exercise 79: Take the Pop Quiz!

1. true

2. true

3. A

4. true

5. B

6. B

7. D

8. true

9. C

10. false

Fluency

Exercise 84: Syllables Are Key!

- finger
- target
- window
- horseshoe
- tiger
- single
- regain
- forget
- depart
- misplace

Exercise 85: Go with What You Know

- ex/termon/ting
- mis/pleas/ted
- pre/trock/ed
- in/just/ed
- mid/forst/ed
- re/plocat/ing
- in/kick/est
- un/strold/ing
- clart/ing
- blart/ed
- tras/tion
- plomp/ing
- in/quest/or
- di/verst/er
- jimp/er
- glost/ment
- froft/ed
- hilm/est
- clert/ing
- exampl/in/a/tion
- re/crost/ing

Exercise 88: Give Me a Break!

The/African/leopard/can/show/a/great/deal/of/variation/in/coat/color/. This/depends/on/where/it/is/located/. This/is/called/the/habitat/. The/color/of/the/African/leopard's/coat/varies/from/a/pale/yellow/to/a/deep/gold/. There/are/also/black/leopards/. Male/leopards/are/usually/larger/than/females/. Some/mountain/leopards/are/smaller/and/less/heavy/than/other/leopards/but/all/leopards/usually/hunt/at/night.

Exercise 98: Matching Phrases

- The teacher told the class to sit because they needed to take attendance.
- The pizza was hot and extremely spicy.
- The senate refused to discuss the bill, for it had been in the House of Representatives for the last two years.
- The weather was cooperating, yet it still felt like it might rain.
- The doctor lost his tongue depressor but was able to examine the patient's tonsils without it.
- The young child was very tired, so her mother put her to bed very early.
- The printer was stuck, but eventually it printed out the document.
- The man read the newspaper while his wife watched the news.
- The student went to the café after the last bell rang at the end of the day.
- I love dark chocolate, and I like milk chocolate as well.
- The student got very upset because he received a bad grade on his math test.

- The young girl disliked reading, but she loved to create and write short stories.
- The young married couple decided to move to another country, so they had to get new passports and work visas.
- The movie ending was so good, and the good guys won in the end.
- She is very nice and personable, yet I still don't completely trust her.
- Tim decided not to wait because his friend was over an hour and a half late.
- The 211 bus didn't show up, so I caught the 212 bus and was home earlier.

Reading-Comprehension Activities

Exercise 100: Understanding Reading Comprehension

1. It is a pilgrimage and a challenge, and it will give them time to reflect on what they want to do at college.

2. They are walking the Camino in Spain. They intend to walk the final section of the route called the Camino Frances.

3. They are in Santiago in Spain.

4. They flew from New York to Barcelona and took a bus to Sarria in northern Spain. They are going to walk the Camino for 10 days.

Exercise 101: Dig This!

1. It means it is something they are very interested in and are very motivated to do, perhaps because they are good at it or just enjoy it.

2. The groups that lived there were the Anglo-Saxons, the Vikings, and the Normans.

3. A relic is a special historical object. The examples in the passage are jewelry, Viking brooches and ornaments, and long boats.

4. It is thought the Norse hall dated from the 10th to 12th century, and it is thought it was used by a high-status ruler.

5. A saga is a historical story. It can be a legend, but it usually tells a story from the ancient past.

6. This means it is passed on from person to person and may not be totally true; it may have changed over time.

7. The accounts were passed on by word of mouth and were written down centuries later. So, it was not surprising that people had different accounts.

Exercise 103: The Ship of Dreams

1. It was believed to be the greatest and most unsinkable ship ever to take to the waters.

2. The walls separating the compartments were only a few feet above the waterline, and if the ship tilted, water could pour from one compartment to another, which is exactly what happened. The builders were overconfident that the ship was unsinkable, and they did not supply enough lifeboats for the passengers.

3. "Complacency" means you are too confident and have not fully checked everything out. An example of this might be thinking you can do your homework in five minutes because you think you know the exercises well, but you have not read through the question sufficiently. Another example might be thinking an exam is going to be easy and not preparing enough for it.

4. It means very scary stories of what happened when the ship was sinking.

5. It is hoped the people can learn from the mistakes of the past and make sea travel safer. It is also a human story of sadness, tragedy, and survival, which is always of interest to people. Additionally, the relics are still on display, so people can go and see them. This, as well as movies made about the *Titanic*, makes it more real.

6. Do not be overconfident, especially when it comes to people's safety. Safety is the most important aspect of any kind of travel.

Exercise 104: What Reading Comprehension Is All About

1. They were there before, it brought back good memories, and the views were breathtaking.

2. He was climbing 2,700 feet uphill, and he was carrying a backpack!

3. The summer is very busy there, and it is too dangerous in the winter.

4. Intermediate refers to the type of walk—a smooth path or a rough path—and whether the hills are very steep and dangerous, which would mean the walkers would need to have a lot of experience and the right type of gear. Intermediate would probably mean you need some experience, but you do not need to be an expert hill climber or walker.

5. "Duo" means two.

6. They were not going to be able to see each other for some time because they were going to different parts of the country.

7. Yosemite Falls is in Yosemite National Park.

8. "No Campfires" and "No Dogs Allowed Beyond This Point."

9. Campfires can easily get out of control and result in danger and destruction. Dogs can wander away from their owners and can get lost and have, or cause, an accident.

10. Many families go on summer vacation when school is out.

Resources

Websites

Celebrities with Dyslexia: WebMD.com/children/ss/slideshow-celebrities-dyslexia

List of Dyslexic Achievers: Dyslexia.com/about-dyslexia/dyslexic-achievers/all-achievers

Famous People with Dyslexia: Blog.Ongig.com/diversity-and-inclusion/famous-people-with-dyslexia

Tips from Students with Dyslexia: Dyslexia.Yale.edu/resources/dyslexic-kids-adults/tips-from-students

Ready-to-Use Materials (mainly for teachers): Dyslexia-and-literacy.international

21 Super Strategies to Ensure Success at School by Liz Dunoon: HelpingChildrenWith Dyslexia.com

Assistive Technology for Dyslexia: ReadingRockets.org/article/assistive-technology-kids-learning-disabilities-overview

Information on Dyslexia: Understood.org/en/learning-attention-issues/child-learning-disabilities/dyslexia/understanding-dyslexia

Information on Dyslexia and Reading: CallScotland.org.uk/information/dyslexia/reading, and Dysguise.com

Books

From Talking to Writing: Strategies for Supporting Narrative and Expository Writing by Terrill M. Jennings and Charles W. Haynes

The Study Skills Handbook by Stella Cottrell

200 Tricky Spellings in Cartoons: Visual Mnemonics for Everyone by Lidia Stanton

Evergreen: A Guide to Writing with Readings by Susan Fawcett

Words Their Way with Struggling Readers: Word Study for Reading, Vocabulary, and Spelling Instruction, Grades 4-12 by Kevin Flanigan, Latisha Hayes, Shane Templeton, Donald Bear, Marcia Invernizzi, and Francine Johnson

The Big Book of Dyslexia Activities for Kids and Teens by Gavin Reid, Nick Guise, and Jennie Guise

References

Achieve More Reading Center. "The Gold Standard." Accessed April 12, 2021. AchieveMoreReading.com/the-gold-standard.

International Dyslexia Association. "Definition of Dyslexia." Accessed April 12, 2021. DyslexiaIDA.org/definition-of-dyslexia.

Understood. "11 Methods for Teaching Reading That Help Struggling Readers." Reading Rockets. Accessed April 12, 2021. ReadingRockets.org/article/11-methods-teaching-reading-help-struggling-readers.

About the Authors

Dr. Gavin Reid is an international psychologist and author. He was formerly a classroom teacher and a university lecturer at the University of Edinburgh in the UK. He has written over 40 books in the field of dyslexia, learning skills, and motivation. His books have been translated into seven languages.

Dr. Reid is passionate about helping to achieve equal opportunities for those with dyslexia and other learning differences and is a strong advocate of the strengths and positive aspects of dyslexia. His website is DrGavinReid.com. He resides in Vancouver, Canada.

Jenn Clark is a certified structured literacy practitioner with a private teaching practice in the Orton-Gillingham approach in Vancouver, Canada. A certified primary school teacher, EAL instructor, and a multisensory language education (MSLE) instructor, Jenn also holds a BA in English from the University of Western Ontario and a Certificate of Competence in Educational Testing (CCET). She has spent the past 10 years teaching students with learning differences as well as supporting parents.

She is co-creator of Aduri, a mindfulness program for young children, and has co-authored several books on reading fluency, spelling, and writing. Learn more at TheLitGroup.ca.

9 781648 769214